I0085764

GEEKS ON A MISSION

In Their Own Words

ALEX HILLS, EDITOR

© 2013 Alex Hills and others.
Chapter 1 © 2013 Alex Hills
Chapter 2 © 2013 Hermona Tamrat
Chapter 3 © 2013 Alimou Bah
Chapter 4 © 2013 Kathryn Dickens McKissick
Chapter 5 © 2013 Adrienne White
Chapter 6 © 2013 Yixin Liu
Chapter 7 © 2013 Joseph Mertz

All rights reserved

No part of this publication may be reproduced, stored in a retrieval system, or transmitted, in any form or by any means, electronic, mechanical, photocopying, recording, or otherwise, without the written permission of the author.

First published by Dog Ear Publishing
4010 W. 86th Street, Ste H
Indianapolis, IN 46268
www.dogearpublishing.net

ISBN: 978-1-4575-2-174-4

This book is a work of non-fiction based on actual events. The editor, authors and publisher make no explicit guarantee as to the accuracy of the information contained in the book, although every effort has been made to be as historically authentic and error-free as possible.

This book is printed on acid-free paper.

Printed in the United States of America

For the families who nurtured and inspired these students

CONTENTS

ACKNOWLEDGMENTS

Here you will read about some interesting and unusual people. When they were students at Carnegie Mellon University, they volunteered to use their skills to help developing nations — and they had some remarkable experiences along the way. These (now former) students tell their stories in these pages. They are:

- Hermona Tamrat, a civil engineering student from Silver Spring, Maryland,

- Alimou Bah, a graduate student in information systems management from Conakry, the capital city of the African nation of Guinea,

- Kathryn (Kayt) Dickens, a graduate student in public policy and management from Fremont, California,

- Adrienne White, a graduate student in network security from Jonesboro, Louisiana, and

- Yixin Liu, an electrical and computer engineering student from Singapore.

All have generously given their time to write chapters for this book. Professor Joseph Mertz of Carnegie Mellon has also written a chapter describing the program that allowed these students, and many others, to work in developing nations.

Thanks to Professor Mertz and the five students whose stories follow. I also thank my wife Meg, daughters Karen and Rebecca, Greg Moore, Imke Lehmann, and Matthew Murry for their advice, assistance, and, most of all, patience.

— Alex Hills, Editor

Distinguished Service Professor

Carnegie Mellon University

June 2013

CHAPTER ONE

ARRIVAL 2012

ALEX HILLS

The pitch of the jet engines dropped as the pilot throttled back to begin the descent. Soon we were on final approach with flaps and gear down and ready for landing. Meanwhile on the ground a university student was waiting. She was working in a land far from her university and far from her home. I hadn't yet met her, but we had a common goal.

She was one of a group of unusual students studying at one of the world's best universities. Their university had helped them develop professional skills highly valued in the job market. They were students of information technology and engineering.

The students had worked hard to get to the university, and they had accumulated debt along the way. It's an expensive place to go to school. Lucrative employment beckoned. They could have been well compensated at summer jobs on Wall Street or in Silicon Valley. But their skills were also needed by others without the money to pay them. So the students were donating their summer vacations to work in far off places. They were volunteering, working on projects they considered important.

These young professionals were smart, talented, educated, and, most important, motivated to help solve important problems. All worked without fanfare to do good things. They were typical of a new breed.

All were students of Carnegie Mellon University, a place that has distinguished itself as a world-class institution. But this same university also offers its students a chance to use their newly acquired skills to help people in developing nations around the world.

The students work as professional consultants, peers to the top people in client organizations, often non-governmental organizations or government agencies. And, for many of the students, it's their first real-world professional experience. The clients get top-notch professional assistance, and the students get an experience not available in any classroom. Everyone wins.

The student volunteers usually, but not always, work in teams of two or more. They develop and improve their communication skills by writing reports and making frequent oral presentations. These are important skills for working professionals but ones that are not always emphasized in a university education.

When the consulting projects are complete, clients are thrilled with the results. But the students are happy, too. They've had the benefit of living and working in a foreign country, immersed in exotic languages and cultures. And they've done important work. Very important work. Some students say "this was the best part of my university education." Others say it was a life-changing experience that changed the direction of their careers and even their lives.

This is a new breed of young professional. They are out to change the world.

Officially called "Technology Consulting in the Global Community," it's an unusual program. Founded and directed by Carnegie Mellon's Professor Joseph Mertz, the program has been sending student volunteer consultants to developing nations for nine years. So far 76 students have worked with 35 organizations in 14 developing nations around the world.

In the pages that follow, five of these student volunteers tell their stories. They describe their childhoods and early life experiences. They explain the events that led them to volunteer to work in remote parts of the world. And they tell how their volunteer experiences later influenced their lives.

Initially each was encouraged by Professor Mertz to undertake a summer consulting project in a faraway place. Some had taken his course, titled "Technology Consulting in the Community." All had been through an intensive orientation covering the consulting techniques and methods they would use, along with some real-world practical information on how to survive — and thrive — in a developing nation. Professor Mertz launched each of them on an international adventure. He inspired them all.

And I'm lucky to have helped all of the young volunteers whose words appear in this book. I worked with them and advised them in advance of their departure from the United States, visited them at their job sites, and counseled them throughout their projects as they formulated and presented work results to their clients.

The projects start early each spring, when Joe and I work with prospective clients around the world to help them sort out their consulting needs. Then we screen applications from students who want to work on projects, and we pair the students' skills with clients' needs. Matches are made, and, late in the spring, we help students prepare for their projects.

Before they even leave the United States, students are taught about our consulting approach. They will not just be interns — they will be real consultants who must establish and maintain strong, professional relationships with their clients, also called "community partners."

Students usually arrive in their host countries in late May. After they settle into summertime housing that has been arranged for them by their clients, work on their projects begins. The first order of business is to help the client clearly define the problem at hand. A clear definition of the problem is needed before a solution can be sought.

Clients must have a strong commitment to work with the student consultants. We ask a senior executive of each client organization to be the client representative, supervising the project and spending at least two to three hours per week working with the consultants. When I make a site visit, I meet with the client representative to confirm his or her commitment to work with the consultants in this way because this kind of client-consultant interaction is critical to a project's success.

By the time I arrive on-site, the team has already started to work on problem definition, that critical first step in the consulting process. Without our consulting model, there would be a natural tendency to skip directly to a solution before even discussing what the problem really is. It takes discipline to avoid this pitfall. Consultants and client representatives must first work together to understand and define the problem, even if it takes a while.

Critical to our consulting model are its core concepts of *capacity building* and *sustainability*. The developing nation landscape is littered with well-meant projects that have been unsustainable — projects whose good works don't last much beyond the departure of their well-meaning proponents.

Our consultants' goal is not to solve the problem by themselves but to work with the client to solve the problem in a way that gives the client a new capacity to sustain the solution after the consultants have left. Building this sustainability begins with creating a personal rapport between client and consultant, and it continues with an agreement on what the problem really is. The client is involved in the project from the beginning and influences its development as it unfolds.

Sustainability also depends on building capacity, the ability of the client organization to use and maintain the new system or make improvements after the consultants' departure. Students spend many hours training client personnel on how to use and maintain what they have built together.

Early in each project, after the students have a little "settling in" time, a professor — usually Joe, me, or our colleague, Professor Randy Weinberg — drops in to visit the newly minted consultants for three or four days. We want to be sure that things have started out well, that both client and consultants are on their way to a detailed project plan, and that housing and other living arrangements are adequate. Housing is never fancy, but it meets basic needs. On the same visit we confirm that a senior executive has committed the time needed to work with the student consultants.

As you will read in the students' stories that follow, there are often small — or even big — things a visiting professor can do at this early stage to help a project start off well. Joe, Randy and I provide a framework within which these amazing young people can work. And we provide advice and encouragement as they develop a game plan for their work and then carry out that plan.

But we only give advice. These young people just need an opportunity to spread their wings. Then they go on and get the job done. And, when they come home at the end of the summer, they have both grateful clients and a new perspective on their lives and careers.

You are about to meet five interesting people — and read about their lives before they volunteered to help in developing nations, their experiences working abroad, and their later reflections on what they learned.

These are their stories.

CHAPTER TWO

PERU 2012

HERMONA TAMRAT

I arrived in Pucallpa before the sun. Around 6am. As I struggled to keep my eyes open, I walked up the aisle, and exited the jet. "Bienvenido a Pucallpa," said the air hostess as a warm hospitable smile spread across her face. I took the first step down the air stairs, enveloped in a blanket of humidity distinct from any I had experienced before. I had lived through nineteen District of Columbia summers in my swamp city with an average humidity of "too-humid-for-Hermona," but this was *humid*. I took a look around and saw a light fog hovering over acres of thick, tall grasses surrounding me on all sides. Roots and grasses had encroached on the tarmac with such persistence that its edges were cracked and broken, creating a jagged border between black pavement and green plant life.

Welcome to the jungle, Hermona.

Before my summer in Peru, I thought of "volunteering" in one specific way, a way that pertained primarily, if not only, to the three pillars of life: food, water, and shelter. So I volunteered. I participated in several "Homeless Walkathons" in D.C. and dedicated evenings to soup kitchens, school services trips, and other similar activities. I was educated in the D.C. Catholic school system, from first grade all the way through high school, and a specified number of hours of "community service" were required each year. So volunteering has always had a presence in my life, but it was just a means to an end — like passing 6th grade. That is not to say I didn't enjoy volunteering or see the value in volunteering. I did. But if it were not a school requirement, I probably wouldn't have chosen to volunteer as frequently.

So how does that girl find herself spending the summer in Nicaragua and Peru seven years later, volunteering rather than interning like every other sensible Carnegie Mellon student?

It all started with a phone call. But not quite so dramatic.

My good friend and now "big time" consultant Marlen Amaro called me one day when I was studying in Hunt Library. She told me that her professor, Joseph Mertz, was looking for students with interest in working for the Technology Consulting in the Global Community (TCinGC) program in Peru. He needed students with Spanish language skills.

I had met Marlen my freshman year, but we became friends early in my junior year, 2011-2012, because we were both members of SIFE: Nicaragua. SIFE stands for Students in Free Enterprise. It's a service organization with volunteer projects in Pittsburgh and in Rosa Grande, Nicaragua. We worked together with other SIFE members to create Microsoft Office tutorials to present to the teachers of Rosa Grande in May of 2012.

Were it not for Marlen's call I would not have contacted Professor Mertz or applied to TCinGC. I owe my amazing summer in Pucallpa to her. Thanks, Marlen.

I had heard about TCinGC previously. Every year the Carnegie Mellon Office of International Education holds an information session about working and volunteering abroad. I had attended every info session that was held, but my summer plans never went in that direction. TCinGC was one of the most intriguing volunteer programs described in the sessions. Students work in developing nations as full time volunteer consultants for ten weeks with a "partner" organization. Together with the partner, students define the problem, or opportunity, that the organization is facing and design a consulting project with a "scope of work" and work schedule to be carried out through the summer. I had been impressed by the collaborative nature of the volunteer work and the great responsibility that these student consultants took on. After speaking with Marlen, I emailed Professor Mertz to set up a meeting with him and start the application process. And, once the ball was set in motion, it didn't stop until I found myself in the city of Pucallpa, Peru.

Pucallpa sits in the jungle at the edge of the Ucayali River.

⊕

It was hard to believe. I was really in the Amazon jungle. *The Amazon.* It had been 22 hours since I left the Baltimore-Washington International Airport. The first order of business: sleep. I am one of those Carnegie Mellon anomalies that do not pull two all-nighters each week. I like my sleep. I always have. You could always count on me to be the child that fell asleep in a restaurant or at the New Year's Eve party at 8:30pm because that was my bedtime. I never understood why kids hated bedtime. I am a full supporter of bedtime. So it seemed appropriate that my time in Pucallpa started with a nap and a shower.

For my consulting project, my primary contact was Rafael Azerrad, the director of the school where I worked. It's called Colegio Antonio Raimondi. Rafael and his wife Wendy took me to lunch, showed me around the school campus, introduced me to some teachers and staff members, and helped me buy some groceries and house supplies. They took care of me throughout all of my first week until I felt comfortable and settled into my new environment. Rafael and Wendy had once left Pucallpa to live in Israel for a few years. They told me about their first week of living in Israel and how difficult it was for them to be in a new city where they knew no one.

Rafael and Wendy could not have been more gracious and generous, and I am so grateful to them. They have two children, Triana and Rafaela, who are 6 and 3 years old. I got to know them quite well during my first week or two. Cute and full of life, they brought a sense of familiarity to my life in Pucallpa, especially in my first few days. I like to be around young children. I have lots of cousins so it was a familiar space. My mother is the oldest of 14 siblings, most of whom are married with children and live in Silver Spring, Maryland, like me, all within about ten miles of our house. We are all close — both physically and emotionally.

Rafael explained the *colegio's* structure to me in one of our first meetings.

I had been lucky. I'd traveled to other countries for vacation or studies, but on those trips there was always a familiar element. Moving to Pucallpa was the first time that everything surrounding me was new and every experience was a first. From the smells that filled me as I drove through the streets to the apartment I would call home for the next ten weeks. From the people I would see and work with each day to the tastes and textures of foods. It was overwhelming and exhilarating and frightening and exciting and humbling and more than I could have hoped for.

I had arrived in Pucallpa Tuesday morning after a nearly full day of travelling, but I was in the office Wednesday morning, ready to charge forward with my work. The first two weeks were all about observing and understanding every aspect of the school and, just as important, forming strong relationships with the director, Rafael, his mother and the school founder, Cecilia Urrutia, and as many teachers and staff members as possible.

Pucallpa had an appealing central area.

Rafael and Cecilia made the process easy for me. I could not have asked for warmer or more hospitable partners.

But this first task wasn't as easy as I anticipated. I had come to Colegio Antonio Raimondi in the middle of the school year and everyone was, of course, in their groove while I was trying to find my footing in the thick Amazon grass. It was difficult for me to find a balance between taking charge of the task at hand and not feeling like I was intruding on the already established rhythm of the school. But I had to put aside my shyness and push myself. Most TCinGC projects had at least two volunteer consultants per site, but I was a team of one. I didn't have a coworker with whom to consult, collaborate, and get support. Despite my many class readings on working across cultures, no theory truly and fully prepares you for practice. I knew and anticipated all the workplace adjustments that I would face moving to Pucallpa, but knowing it is different from living it.

As the days passed and Pucallpa gradually became my new home, some of the 'newness' began to fade. I was becoming more familiar with the city, diving into my work and settling into my apartment. But, as the newness wore off, a bit of fear started to creep in. I had never lived on my own. I had traveled extensively, but never alone. Living on my own without any of my friends or family was tough. But I found comfort in something I didn't like at home: routine.

I began to *love* routine. I went to bed and woke up at the same time every day. I ate the same breakfast of cereal and black coffee every morning while watching the TV Peru sports news. It happened that the 20 minutes I ate breakfast coincided with that 20 minute sports segment. I stuck to the same work schedule every day, including my daily Skype sessions with my Dad. And, after work, I came home and tried to catch *Fresh Prince of Bel Air* dubbed over in Spanish. Routine became something familiar, something stable that I could hold on to in an environment where I often felt I had little control. And one part of my daily routine that led indirectly to my favorite part of Pucallpa was lunch.

Every day for lunch I bought food at the school from the *señora* who ran the kiosk. She was a kind woman with a sharp tongue. She told dirty jokes. And she made great food. My second week in Pucallpa she asked if I wanted to have a meeting with her friend Gilberto Panduro, the head of the language department at the university. She thought it might be good if I taught some English classes in the evenings. I began to tell her that I wasn't qualified or trained to be an English teacher, but she wouldn't hear it. She was already dialing his number before I finished my sentence. I decided to go ahead and meet with Gilberto, because, even if I chose not to teach, it couldn't hurt to meet another *Pucallpino*. What the hell, what did I have to lose? So she set up a meeting for me that afternoon.

After work I took a *mototaxi* back to the university and headed for the language department. A *mototaxi* is a sort of modified motorcycle, with a high seat for one or two passengers behind the driver and under a canopy. Up to that point, Rafael had driven me to and from the school because it was on his way home. But I decided to start taking a *mototaxi* from the university to the school because I was beginning to feel comfortable with the city. The first time riding in a *mototaxi*, I thought I broke it. The engine was so loud and the seat car vibrated so vigorously that I was sure that I wouldn't make it back to my apartment. I mentally prepared myself for a mechanical breakdown at any moment. But I really had nothing to worry about. I later learned that every *mototaxista* is also an amateur mechanic and can fix their *mototaxi* at any time. Breakdowns are normal. You simply hop off and flag down the next available motorcar, which is typically a few feet behind you.

Mototaxis like this one gave me some exciting rides.

The *mototaxi* reached such speeds that my "click-it-or-ticket" trained mind imagined the trajectory of my unbelted body after a crash. As we drove further from the city center, I was in for a treat. The side streets perpendicular to the main avenues were not paved. I remember a few moments when I was airborne, hovering above the seat after speeding over a large rock jutting out from the ground.

Soon I was at the gate of the university of the Universidad Nacional de Pucallpa — which all the cool kids called UNU (pronounced OO-noo). I paid the driver five *soles* (I later learned this was too much. Friends told me to refuse to pay more than three *soles*.) Only after getting down from the *mototaxi* did I realize how tense my entire body was. I tried to relax every muscle in my body.

After I was physically able, I walked to the language department. The meeting with Gilberto was really just getting to know each other. I told him my background and why I was in Pucallpa, and he shared his story with me. Gilberto was a native of Pucallpa but had spent lots of time in the U.S. He told me of his need for an English language tutor for a group of students, mostly in high school. They were enrolled in evening sessions to improve their conversational English skills. He was unconcerned about my lack of experience. We spoke for nearly an hour, just swapping stories. Then he asked me if I wanted to meet the students and try teaching the class.

"Sure," I said.

"*Bueno*. Let's go."

"Now?!"

"Yes. Class starts at six," he said as he looked up at the clock that read 6:15pm.

I opened my mouth to protest. I didn't think I should teach the class today, or *any* day, and I had no material for the students.

15

But he seemed to have complete confidence in me, so why didn't I?

At that moment I remembered a quote that I had written down just before leaving home for Peru. I was watching one of my favorite shows, *Inside the Actors Studio*, which airs on the guiltiest of guilty pleasure channels, Bravo. It was the Natalie Portman episode and she said something that resonated with me as I was about to embark on my journey to Pucallpa. She said, "You learn the most by doing things you didn't think you could do. You grow by doing things that scare you." This was an opportunity to learn and grow. So I stopped myself from doing what was safe and went for it. What the hell, what did I have to lose other than a missed opportunity?

"Let's go!" I said to Gilberto, maybe a bit too emphatically, having just had a mini-revelation.

I had a good relationship with my friend Routine since my arrival in Pucallpa, but I had just made one of my best spontaneous decisions ever. Teaching the English class turned out to be my favorite part of life in Pucallpa.

My class was made up primarily of high school students, but there was also a group of about ten university students who occasionally attended. I taught three times a week for two hours each day. I planned the class and prepared the material with complete freedom and flexibility. At the first class we spent time getting to know each other. They asked me questions about life and culture in the U.S., and I asked them the same about Peru. Interestingly, I also recognized the same stereotypical classroom roles in Peru that I had seen at home. There was the troublemaker in the back who wasn't a great English speaker, the outspoken, sweet girl who was clearly top of the class, the jokester that always distracted the class but was sweet and put in real effort, the shy girl who was scared to ask for a little extra help, and the quiet boy who was a shockingly brilliant English speaker. The two-hour class flew by in a flash. This was going to be a breeze, I thought to myself.

✦

But I was in Pucallpa primarily to work as a consultant at Colegio Antonio Raimondi. I had spent the first week asking hundreds of questions, learning as much as I could about the information and management systems in place at the school, and meeting as many of the teachers as possible. I had lots of information collected for my organizational assessment report, but I still didn't feel that I had a handle on what the scope of my work would be. The school had a large number of problems that were more than I could handle in just two months. It was daunting, and I felt a bit uneasy. It was the perfect time for my adviser, Dr. Alex Hills, to pay a visit to Pucallpa.

Exactly one week after I landed in Pucallpa, Dr. Hills came for a short three-day site visit. One part of TCinGC is a short site visit by the student consultant's adviser. I was lucky to have Dr. Hills as my adviser. I had communicated with him via email and phone before leaving for Pucallpa in preparation for the trip, but I had never met him in person. I think Rafael was shocked by this fact. It was only when we were at the airport waiting for Dr. Hills to arrive that I mentioned to him that I wasn't sure what Dr. Hills looked like. It was pretty silly because I could have easily Googled his image. What were the odds that I, a Carnegie Mellon student, and Dr. Hills, a Carnegie Mellon professor, would meet for the first time in Peru? Rafael said that Dr. Hills told him to look for a very tall, slim, white-haired man with glasses. The description was more than sufficient. We were at a domestic airport in Peru where the people are on average a foot shorter than Dr. Hills. We had no difficulty finding him as passengers and their family members flooded the airport's main terminal. It was nice to finally match a face to Dr. Hills' voice.

Dr. Hills' plane landed late in the evening, so we had our first meeting the following morning. Rafael gave him a tour of the campus. As we passed through the *Escuela Inicial*, equivalent to pre-K and kindergarten in the US school system, Rafael's youngest daughter Rafaela ran by and called out "*Prima Hermona!*" (which translates to cousin Hermona). Dr. Hills looked at me and said "Wow, already promoted to cousin by the kids. You're settling in pretty well, it seems!" I admit: I was beaming. It felt good to be validated by a three year old. I was no longer a stranger to Pucallpa, and I was also no longer a stranger in Colegio Antonio Raimondi.

The outdoor spaces of the colegio were quiet
when classes were in session.

After Rafael gave Dr. Hills the full tour of the school, we went back to my office and got down to business. I shared my findings and my concerns about defining and outlining what my

The outdoor spaces were jammed between classes
and at the end of the school day.

project work would entail. We had a few ideas, but things were not clear cut until Rafael joined the meeting. He shared the same information with Dr. Hills that he had already shared with me, but there was one other, more important part. Rafael said that his mother Cecilia was reaching retirement age and would soon stop working at the school, but the future leadership plans had not been decided, or even discussed. When Rafael said this, Dr. Hills had an "ah-ha" look on his face as he saw the most important problem and how I could address it.

We were then able to flesh out what consulting work I would provide for the school. I would work as a management consultant for the school, steering them toward a succession plan for the family business. It would be best to do this years before Cecilia's retirement. Although I didn't have work experience in this field, Dr. Hills had management experience, and he was confident of my ability to carry out the task. And that gave me confidence.

I began to search for available family business succession models, and there were many. I spent more time understanding the structure of the business and the source of its challenges. This allowed me to focus on the succession models most appropriate for the *colegio* and most likely to be successful. In my meeting with Rafael at the end of that week, I learned that his siblings would all be coming to Pucallpa for a vacation and a family reunion. His sisters live in Lima, and his brother lives in Ireland, so it was a rare opportunity to have the whole family together. I immediately thought this reunion would be an opportune time to give a presentation to the whole family, the primary stakeholders in the business.

The consulting model that TCinGC follows is similar to the model that Professor Mertz teaches in his "Technology Consulting in the Community" course at Carnegie Mellon. During our pre-departure orientation, all of us student consultants had a crash course in sustainable consulting. One of the key aspects was seeing every problem as an opportunity. Although this seemed a small distinction, it made a big difference to how I approached my work in Pucallpa. This family reunion was a great opportunity to bring forward an issue that was obvious but had been deferred in the past. But the literature on family business succession planning implores families to do the opposite. Planning should begin early to reduce the risk associated with a leadership transition. So Rafael and I scheduled my presentation to the family to be done during the upcoming reunion.

With three weeks to go, I had a hard, short-term deadline to meet. I was a bit nervous. I had to give a presentation in Spanish on a pretty heavy subject. Although Rafael and all of his siblings speak English very well, Cecilia and her husband Alberto do not. It was imperative that all family members fully understand all of my presentation. In the coming weeks, I emailed Dr. Hills at least once a day. He probably got tired of it, but he never admitted it.

He had worked as a management consultant, so he understood my work as well as I did. He offered great advice. Most often my daily emails were just updates on my work and my next steps. Working alone on a project with new subject matter was daunting. It was difficult to trust myself and my decisions. So these short little emails helped to assure me that I was moving in the right direction. When working with a team, you have others to bounce ideas and work through questions, but, in this case, I had to rely on myself for that assurance, validation, and critical assessment.

Before I knew it, the three weeks were up! They seemed to have passed even faster than the first three weeks, and it was now time to give the presentation to Cecilia, her husband Alberto, Rafael, and his three siblings. I had prepared and rehearsed, but that didn't stop the nerves. I have never liked getting up in front of a group. When I was younger, I studied classical piano and entered annual competitions, but, even with years of experience, I was always nervous until the moment I hit the first key.

In Peru it was no different. I was giving a 20 to 30 minute presentation *in Spanish* about the future of a family's business! *This was big*! But this was also why I decided to take on this project in the first place: to take on a serious challenge and offer my skills to an organization making a big difference in a community.

I woke up that morning before the sun, as I did each morning, with the presentation running through my head. Half asleep and walking in the dark, I opened the door and shrieked at what was before me. *A frog! Nay, two frogs! There was another in the corner!* In my apartment! I froze like an idiot thinking, "Maybe if I don't move they won't see me." I then slowly slinked against the wall towards the bathroom. "No quick movements," I kept saying to myself. I had made it to the bathroom. In one piece. Free from amphibian attack. *Sigh of relief. But now I have two frogs in my apartment, what do I do, what do I do, what do I do??* I first tried to shoo them out towards the door but they just hopped under the couch and out of sight. Great. I then did what any sensible college student would do: ignore it and leave it for later.

The harrowing experience behind me for the moment, I had a major presentation to deliver. In my presentation I spent time discussing the underlying importance of why the family should create a succession plan for the business. Cecilia had built the school from the ground up, and, for Colegio Antonio Raimondi to continue serving Pucallpa's youth, a succession plan was paramount. It was important that they see the necessary next step without my dictating it to them. After presenting a number of models that could guide the family, I focused on the two that I felt best fit their business. Then came a long discussion. The most surprising thing was how quickly they came to agreement. They immediately began to articulate their thoughts and feelings while still being sensitive to their mother's feelings. In their discussion they balanced family and business relationships. It seemed each had been thinking of this for years but had never openly raised the subject. It was too easy to push it aside for later. But the time had finally come. For about 45 minutes, the family talked among themselves about the future of the school, their concerns, their aspirations, and their future goals. Together we revisited one of the two models highlighted in my presentation, and we went through the steps in more detail.

As I left for my apartment after the meeting, I couldn't wipe the huge smile from my face. I could not have been happier with the family's reaction. I did not have to struggle to convince them of the need for a succession plan. This had been my biggest concern heading into the meeting. They immediately understood and, more importantly, agreed with my presentation. I had achieved a major goal in my project.

That night at my English class, I was in an extra good mood, and my students could tell. Instead of the usual lesson, I prepared

Cecilia liked my work on succession planning.

instead for us to listen to English language songs and try to make out the lyrics and meanings. One student, Cesar, asked if he could bring in his guitar to the next class and play English songs like Green Day (his favorite band). I chuckled, but I loved the idea. Each class from then on we spent the last 20 minutes or so singing songs, both in English and Spanish. Over the weeks, teaching my English class became my favorite part of living in Pucallpa. That was also due to the kindness and generosity of Gilberto, the head of the language department. Even when he barely knew me, he trusted me. A native of Pucallpa who had lived all over the United States, he knew how it felt to be an outsider. He always told his students to be hospitable to foreigners, show them kindness, and show them the beauty of Peru through their actions. He served as a wonderful mentor and friend while I was in Pucallpa. I hope he knows how grateful I am.

I'm so lucky to have had the chance to work at Colegio Antonio Raimondi, and I hope that I was able to facilitate the start of a long partnership between TCinGC and the school. They are such a kind, generous, and hardworking family. I wish them all the best. I hope they continue with their plans to pursue a succession plan for the next couple years as Cecilia plans to pass on the leadership of the school. The school provides so many children of Pucallpa the opportunity for a better future. Being a part of that institution, even for ten short weeks, was a wonderful experience.

Here I am with some of the great friends I made in Pucallpa.
Left to right, Rosa, me, Dick and Naysha

As for the frogs (Mr. and Mrs. Kermit), after many failed shoo-ing attempts I decided to leave them alone and coexist harmoniously in the apartment . They were harmless. Besides, I had never had a pet before.

⊕

Leaving Pucallpa was bittersweet. I missed everyone back home and couldn't wait to see them. But I had made a home in Peru, too. I had made wonderful friends, I had lived in a beautiful place, and I had been surrounded by such kind people. My ten weeks in Pucallpa had come to an end, and it was time to go home.

At home the first thing everyone asked me was, "Did your Spanish improve?" Truth be told, it didn't. I am a little ashamed to say that it may have even worsened. I was already fairly fluent in Spanish before traveling to Peru, having studied the language for years. And in Peru I had little opportunity to speak Spanish. One of my goals before leaving home was to become a more fluent Spanish speaker. I have always believed that the mark of fluency in a language is the ability to tell a joke. Think about it. Telling a really good, witty joke requires a good handle on a language. Even in English.

But everyone I spoke with in Pucallpa, friends, the school's teachers, and my students, all wanted to practice speaking English. Pucallpa sees very few English speakers from abroad. Everyone I encountered wanted to practice speaking English with me. And, of course, I was happy to oblige. Teachers would often drop by my office to chat and ask questions on English grammar or pronunciation. Sometimes they had questions about the English language that I couldn't answer. These made me question my own grasp of English. (For example, I never realized that the indefinite article "an" is never used before words that begin with "un-" like university or unique. And why is it that you can say 'I like swimming' or 'I like to swim' and 'I prefer swimming' or 'I prefer to swim' *but* 'I enjoy swimming' and not 'I enjoy to swim.' This bothers me to this day, and I have yet to meet someone who can answer the question.) But, even though I spoke little Spanish and still can't turn out a witty joke on the fly, I'd like to think that

I helped some of my students at the university or teachers at Colegio Antonio Raimondi to tell jokes in English.

One of the coolest residual effects of my work in Pucallpa was a trip to Alaska. Thanks to the generosity and hospitality of Dr. and Mrs. Hills, I joined three other former TCinGC consultants for a memorable week there. I was so lucky to meet and befriend some of the most inspiring and passionate like-minded young professionals on this trip: Adrienne, who had worked in Ghana; Yixin, who had worked in Palau; and Alimou, who worked in Rwanda. We arrived in Alaska as strangers but left as four new friends. As an undergraduate student, it was great to meet Carnegie Mellon alumni who were in the work force and finding ways to integrate volunteer work in their lives.

Other than seeing grizzly bears in Denali National Park, feeding baby reindeer, petting a moose, hiking up a mountain (a small mountain, but the trail was categorized as "strenuous", so it still counts in my book), and walking on a glacier, one of the most memorable moments occurred at the hostel where Adrienne, Alimou, Yixin, and I stayed while at Denali National Park. One evening I was in the kitchen, where five young Japanese girls were cooking but having difficulty with a can opener. They spoke almost no English, and I speak no Japanese. When the girls came over to me, I doubted I could help. They communicated through hand gestures that they needed help with the can opener. I showed them that they needed to really clamp down the opener on the can, and I demonstrated, piercing the can. In unison the girls reacted with "Oh"s and "Ah"s. Then I showed them that they needed to twist the side lever so that it would open the can all the way around. Cheering ensued. We all had a good laugh.

More recently I went to dinner with a friend that I work with in *Juntos*, the Carnegie Mellon student organization that serves the Pittsburgh and Nicaraguan communities through volunteer work. She asked me if I saw myself doing any more volunteering after graduation. I had spent a lot of time exploring, researching hundreds of different one- and two-year programs in a variety of locations. For a time I was set on finding a one-year volunteer position for a civil engineer in Africa. But I later decided to go for my master's degree right after graduation so that I can reach my ultimate career goals. I want to design out-of-this-world bridges and buildings for an international company, but I can't envision my life without the strong presence of some type of volunteer or service work. It is something that I know will always be in my life — like a second job. The way I see it, it *is* a second job, a duty and a responsibility that comes with the immense privileges I have been given.

⊕

I was leaving Pucallpa, as early in the morning as when I had arrived, and I couldn't help but keep replaying those words in my head while walking across the tarmac, "You learn the most by doing things you didn't think you could do. You grow by doing things that scare you."

When I left Pucallpa I was the same five-foot five-inch girl that arrived on June 5, barring a tan, a birthday, and maybe a few pounds. But I had grown. So tall.

CHAPTER THREE

RWANDA 2011

ALIMOU BAH

"What brings you to Rwanda?" the customs officer at the Kigali International Airport asked sternly as he examined my passport.

I looked at him through the glass window that separated us and replied "I am visiting the Aga-hozo-Shalom Youth Village."

"Agahozo-Shalom?" he repeated. He wanted more information about the purpose of my visit.

"Yes, it's a high school. I plan to be here in Rwanda for ten weeks."

"And where do you come from?"

"Well, I left the United States to come to Rwanda, but I am from the Republic of Guinea, as my passport shows. I am currently attending a university located in Pittsburgh, in the United States."

While he was checking for my passport's expiration date and putting his stamp in one of its pages, he commented "So you are from Guinea, go to school in the USA, and visiting Rwanda."

I smiled and replied "Yes."

With the formalities completed, I hurried to the baggage claim area. The baggage carousel soon started running. I had packed only one suitcase for my ten-week stay, and, fortunately, it was one of the first ones to arrive on the carousel. I grabbed it and quickly checked to see if it was damaged or if the lock had been broken before I followed the exit signs.

The arrival lobby was not as crowded as I expected. Since Rwanda has only one international airport, just like Guinea, I thought the arrival lobby would be as packed as Guinea's airport, which is called Gbessia. All international planes arriving in Guinea land at Gbessia. From six o'clock in the morning to midnight, Gbessia's arrival lobby is full of travelers and locals ready to be tour guides for anyone who doesn't speak the local dialects. In return, they hope for a tip. But they usually approach only travelers who look like tourists, likely to tip more than Guineans. I was surprised that there was no such activity at the Kigali International Airport.

I looked for Bosco, the driver who was supposed to meet me. I did not know what he looked like. I hoped he would be holding a piece of paper with my name on it. But I didn't see him. It was my first time in Rwanda, I didn't know anyone in Kigali, and I didn't speak Kinyarwanda, the local dialect, fluently. Only when the plane landed in Kigali had I remembered that I didn't have Bosco's cell phone number. I was worried — but not too much — because I had the contact information of the school's director. So, in the worst case, I would just call him.

Still roaming the lobby, I noticed a currency exchange store and, beside it, a MTN shop. About two weeks before leaving for Rwanda, Jin Seop Kim, my teammate for the next ten weeks, and

I had done some general research about the country. We had collected information about the history, the economy, the business environment, the government, the educational system, the society, and the cultural norms of the country. We had even learned some words in Kinyarwanda because we wanted to be prepared to adapt to the Rwandan environment. I remembered that MTN was a South African cell phone service provider operating throughout Rwanda. Their network fully covered the eastern region of Rwanda, and the Agahozo-Shalom school, where I would be working, was in Nunga, a city in the eastern region approximately 30 miles east of Kigali. So Nunga was covered by the MTN cell phone network.

I entered the currency store and exchanged one hundred U.S. dollars for sixty thousand Rwandan francs. Then I went to the MTN shop and bought a SIM card and some prepaid minutes. My Android phone could work on any GSM network, including MTN. I opened the back of my Android phone and inserted the new SIM card. I turned on the phone, dialed in the code from the prepaid card, and loaded five bucks worth of minutes. MTN provided fast data service in Kigali. I was able to directly connect to the Internet though the phone and even receive Twitter feeds. Here I was in East Africa — more than 5,000 miles from the US — and still plugged into my networks. I realized that the world really *is* flat.

As I left the shop, I spotted a man, accompanied by three younger guys and an older woman, arriving in the lobby. He didn't have a sign or a piece of paper with a name on it, but he seemed to be looking for someone. He was trying to make eye contact with anyone holding a suitcase. I walked toward the group and, when he looked at me, I asked "are you from Agahozo-Shalom?"

Bosco smiled and answered *"yego,"* a Kinyarwanda word that I knew. It meant "yes." I was relieved to hear that response. I immediately extended my hand and introduced myself to the entire group. We made our way to the minivan in the parking lot. The drive from the airport to Nunga lasted 45 minutes. It was a Sunday. There was little traffic and only a few pedestrians. The landscape was spectacular. There were hills everywhere — one after another and curvy roads in between. I was in the "land of a thousand hills." I was excited to be there, and I looked forward to the coming ten weeks.

Bosco drove at the speed limit. The minivan's windows were open, and a light breeze flowed through. I sat in the back with the rest of the group. The three younger guys seemed eager to learn about me, but they shied away from asking me questions. So I asked the questions instead and ended up learning more about them. They were all second-year students at the Agahozo-Shalom school, a residential high school. Before picking me up from the airport, they had run the Kigali marathon. They had trained for the marathon for weeks. All three successfully completed the run, and one of them finished in the top ten.

I also chatted with Sika, the woman in the group. She had travelled from Boston to volunteer and live at the school for more than a year. I asked her questions about the school and Rwanda in general. I told her that the country's landscape reminded me of Dalaba, a small town in Guinea that I had often visited. 180 miles west of Guinea's capital, it is also engulfed in rolling hills intertwined with curvy roads. To me the scenery of Rwanda and Dalaba look identical. But the difference was the climate. Rwanda has two rainy and two dry seasons, while Dalaba has only one of each.

Looking surprised to hear the name Dalaba, Sika asked me if Miriam Makeba, the famous South African singer and activist, lived in that small town. In fact, Miriam Makeba did live in Dalaba in the late 1960s and 1970s. She was exiled from South Africa because she had publicly criticized the apartheid government. Her South African citizenship was revoked, but the Republic of Guinea granted her honorary citizenship.

She moved to Dalaba with Stokely Carmichael, her husband at the time. Stokely was also a civil rights activist. In the mid-1960s, he led the Student Nonviolent Coordinating Committee (SNCC) in the United States. But his exile to Guinea was self-imposed. Miriam and Stokely became close to Sékou Touré, then the president of Guinea. They both would later serve as his advisors, and Miriam became Guinea's official delegate to the United Nations.

My mother lived in Dalaba when she was in high school, during the same time as Miriam and Stokely. She told me stories about them when we visited Dalaba and drove around its hills. Sika told me that her father had also lived in Dalaba when he worked for the World Health Organization during the same time as Miriam and Stokely. And that is how she knew about the world famous Miriam Makeba living — some forty years ago — in this unknown small town that resembles Rwanda. What a coincidence!

⊕

My project partner Jin Seop Kim was to arrive in Rwanda the same evening. This was his first time traveling to Africa, and I knew he was excited about the opportunity to visit and work in Rwanda. Jin Seop and I met for the first time at a restaurant in Pittsburgh about a week after we found that we both were admitted into the Technology Consulting in the Global Community (TCinGC) program. Though we were both Carnegie Mellon students, we had never seen each other around campus. We wanted to get to know each other. We would be working together in Rwanda for ten weeks.

We found out that we had a lot in common. We were both the same age and both interested in technology and developing countries. We found volunteering to be satisfying and rewarding. We liked to travel and discover new things. And each of us spoke two languages in addition to English. Jin Seop is from South

Korea, but he had lived in India and China with his family for most of his life. He travelled to the United States in 2006 to attend Carnegie Mellon University. But, after his sophomore year, he went back to South Korea to do his mandatory military service. He served for 21 months, and then returned to Carnegie Mellon to finish his degree. While I was discovering Rwanda with Jin Seop, I also learned about India, China, and South Korea.

I had heard about the TCinGC program from Professor Joe Mertz. I took two classes taught by Professor Mertz. The two classes were Distributed Systems and IT Consulting. Professor Mertz talked about the TCinGC program in both classes. I was thinking about the summer internship required by my graduate program at Carnegie Mellon, and I was hoping to do something out of the ordinary, something challenging and different. I did not want to spend the summer sitting in a cubicle and simply writing software. Been there, done that, I thought. So, when Professor Mertz announced that the TCinGC program had a potential consulting project in Rwanda, I immediately told him of my strong interest in participating in the program and doing a project in Rwanda.

I knew that the TCinGC project in Rwanda would be a great learning opportunity for me. And I knew that the IT consulting class I was taking with Professor Mertz would prepare me very well for the project in Rwanda. After all, he was the TCinGC program director. Further, as part of a semester-long project for his class, I was working with a non-profit organization in Pittsburgh that had just received a federal grant to open four public computer labs in low-income neighborhoods in Pittsburgh. Throughout the semester, I consulted with the organization's executive director and assisted him in choosing technology solutions to address their needs. This consulting engagement taught me how to assess and frame problems and solutions, communicate technical ideas, and manage the client's expectations. But I also knew that the project in Rwanda would help me expand these skills. I would be in a different environment with a different culture and a completely different set of problems.

In addition, I was interested in how different countries in Africa were using technology for development. I knew that African countries couldn't afford to miss the technology advancements that were occurring around the world — in both developed and developing countries. Developing countries in Africa could use the new advancements in technology as both enablers and accelerators of socio-economic development. So I had closely followed in the news the IT policies and projects that countries on the African continent were enacting and implementing. The trip would give me a chance to see first-hand what was happening in Rwanda, technology-wise.

I had attended high school in the state of Maryland. Like most of the high schools in the United States, mine didn't teach courses in African history or literature, even as electives. So when I was in the 11th grade, I started an independent study about African history, literature, and politics, and I continued this independent study throughout my undergraduate years at Morehouse College, though it was unrelated to my computer science major. I did it all on my own time. At the beginning I studied countries in West Africa. I was interested in that region of Africa because it's where Guinea is located.

For most African countries I read about their histories before and during the European colonization of Africa. Only two countries were able to retain some kind of independence during that period. The countries were Ethiopia and Liberia, but even Ethiopia was briefly dominated by the Italians. The colonial "scramble for Africa" put in place the borders that still define most African countries. I also studied the socio-economic and political make-up of the different states, kingdoms, and empires that existed in each region before the "scramble" and learned about heads of state, kings, and emperors who led the fight against European colonization.

Rwanda is located in the great lake region of East Africa. It is bordered by the Democratic Republic of Congo in the west, Uganda in the north, Tanzania in the east, and Burundi in the south. The country gained independence from Belgium in 1962. The current population is approximately ten million, with many young people. Paul Kagame began serving as President of Rwanda in 2000, but he had been the *de facto* leader of the country since 1994.

Rwanda is well known for the genocide that took place there, when more than 800,000 Tutsis and moderate Hutus were killed by extremist Hutus. The assassination of Juvenal Habyarimana, then the Rwandan president, was the catalyst that started the mass killings. His plane was shot down at the Kigali International Airport. It's still a mystery what group carried out this act, but for months the country was in complete chaos. Kagame and his armed forces, known as the Rwandan Patriotic Forces (RPF), ended the genocide when they entered the country from Uganda and took control in July 1994. Kagame and the RPF were welcomed as heroes, and Rwanda has been rebuilding itself since then.

A month after Jin Seop and I came back to Pittsburgh from Rwanda, Kagame visited Carnegie Mellon University. Because we had worked in Rwanda the entire summer, the university invited us to meet and greet him before he offered a keynote address about Rwanda's development strategy.

One of my favorite authors, Thierno Monenembo, who has written many fictional and non-fictional books that depict West Africa throughout the nineteenth and twentieth centuries, wrote an award-winning fictional book, *The Oldest Orphan*, that depicts the Rwandan genocide. The book tells the story of Faustin Nsenghimana, an adolescent who survived the genocide. When

I read the book in 2004, I never imagined that a few years later I would be working as a student consultant for a non-profit organization in Rwanda, an organization that educates and provides life-changing opportunities to those who were orphaned by the genocide.

In *The Oldest Orphan*, Faustin is 15 years old. While he awaits his execution in a prison in Kigali, he narrates the story of his life and the cruelty that took place during and after the genocide. He describes the horrors of war and its heavy cost in human lives. Faustin Nsenghimana's story vividly portrays the chaos that was Rwanda in 1994. The book's narrative comes to my mind whenever civil war or unrest in an African country is mentioned in the news.

A sign announced that we had arrived at ASYV.

Soon after our departure from Kigali we arrived at the Agahozo-Shalom Youth Village (ASYV). The Village had opened in

December 2008 to help educate those who were orphaned by the genocide. Its mission is to "to help the youth who had gone through a time of trauma to be healthy, self-sufficient, and engaged in rebuilding Rwanda." ASYV was founded by Anne Heyman, a South African native who lives in the United States. The residential community, sitting on 144 acres of land, had 375 students and was planning for 500 in the next academic year.

The Village creates a space where the youth "dry their tears" (*Agahozo* in Kinyarwanda) and "live in peace" (*Shalom* in Hebrew) while "restoring the rhythm of life." ASYV has a formal education program led by a principal and teachers and an informal education program led by a residential staff, with each program supporting ASYV's mission. Our consulting assignments during our ten weeks at ASYV allowed Jin Seop and me to interact and engage with the teachers, the residential staff, and the students.

The Village Director was Ilan Blum, an Israeli. He had been at ASYV since 2010. All of the other directors reported to Ilan, who was also the client representative for our project. Jin Seop and I formally met with him at least once a week throughout the project to discuss our progress with our consulting tasks and to communicate the challenges that we faced in completing the tasks. Ilan really believed in our project and wanted it to be successful.

The Agahozo-Shalom students lived in residential houses. All students in a residential house were in the same grade. Each house held a "family." The families were named after famous personalities from Rwanda and around the world. Some of the family names were Alex Kagame, a Rwandan poet and historian, Pakistani political leader Benazir Bhutto, and the civil rights activist Martin Luther King Jr. Each house had a family mother and a counselor. The family mothers provided guidance and advised students on personal matters. They also led the family gatherings that happened almost every evening. The counselors

The Village's residential houses are tucked neatly
into the rolling hills of Rwanda.

acted as older sisters or brothers, mentors, role models and con-
fidantes.

The high school at ASYV is called the Liquidnet Family
High School. Liquidnet is a U.S.-based company that has sponsored and financially supported ASYV since it was founded. And
each year a team of Liquidnet employees travels to Rwanda for a
few days to volunteer at ASYV. During our first week at ASYV,
Jin Seop and I worked closely with the Liquidnet team of volunteers for that year. Liquidnet team members had installed and
maintained ASYV's IT infrastructure. Throughout that week we
helped the Liquidnet team and Mike, a long-term IT support
volunteer living and working in the village. We helped them
replace wireless network equipment, install backup servers, and
provide technical support. The time we spent with the Liquidnet
team during that week allowed us to gain a better understanding

of the technology infrastructure at ASYV. And we would continue working with Mike over our remaining weeks as we worked on our consulting tasks.

During the second week, with the Liquidnet team headed back to the US, Jin Seop and I spent a lot of time talking to Mike. He had completed half of his 12-month stint at ASYV. Previously he had run a summer camp at an environmental education center in Pennsylvania, and he had taught himself IT while he worked there. At ASYV he was the go-to person for anything related to technology. During the short time Mike had been in Rwanda, he had learned a lot about the culture and society.

Market day in the nearby village of Nunga was once a week. People came from surrounding rural areas to an open space in the center of Nunga. Sellers placed their goods on tables, and buyers roamed around looking for the best goods at the best prices. Mike taught us that market day was the best day to purchase the freshest fruits and vegetables. Usually these came straight from the sellers' gardens. In the case of *Amandazis*, which are Rwandan-style doughnuts, they came straight from the sellers' kitchens. Jin Seop and I usually bought a one week supply of *Amandazis*. I often had one or two for breakfast with some coffee or tea. They were great energy boosters, and they also made a good snack during the day.

Mike did not speak Kinyarwanda fluently, but he knew how to navigate the busy market crowd in search of the best prices. Haggling was the norm, and he always bargained — or at least tried to. Mike was the first person to tell us about the meaning of *mzungu*. The term, mostly used in central, eastern and southern Africa, was coined to describe a person of foreign descent. The region's indigenous people initially used it to describe the first European explorers who arrived in the area. Today, any person who is not from the region is labeled a *mzungu*. The term has the same meaning whether spoken in Kinyarwanda or other African languages like Kirundi, Swahili and Lingala, which are spoken in

Burundi, Tanzania and the Democratic Republic of Congo, respectively.

A *mzungu* might have difficulty negotiating prices for goods on market day because the sellers expect a *mzungu* to pay higher than normal prices. Vendors, especially those who sell goods that are hard to find, will likely double or triple their prices before they even start negotiating. In my case, I was lucky because I could easily pass for someone from the region — at least if I didn't try to speak Kinyarwanda too much. If I did, my accent would give me away. So I would always keep the conversation short by just uttering numbers below my highest price limit until a vendor replied "*yego*" or nodded his head in agreement to the price. It always worked!

⊕

Jin Seop and I conducted a lot of interviews with teachers, staff members, and students at ASYV. We hoped that, by talking to them, we would be able to come up with a realistic scope of work for our consulting project. We wanted to understand how information technology was integrated into their daily activities. Before we arrived, ASYV had given us a description of the technology issues that needed attention. But now we were on the ground, and we had only nine more weeks left. Our goal was to be useful and effective within the limited amount of time we had, even if it meant redefining our technology and organizational goals.

Our interviews were usually informal. We tried to make the meetings conversational. We heard from the students and teachers alike that there were not enough computers in the classes. Students also needed to use computers after school to do their homework. But ASYV had only two computer labs. One, at the high school, was used to teach programming, word processing and spreadsheet applications. The other lab was in a learning center located in a residential area. It was primarily used for research, homework and other activities. We heard from Mike

and the staff members that ASYV had recently received a dona-
tion of two hundred computers from South Korea, coincidentally
Jin Seop's home country. The computers had been sitting in a
storage room since they were received. Deo, the computer science teacher at the school, and Mike were capable of installing
the computers, but installing 200 computers could take days,
even with proper planning. Considering their busy schedules —
Deo taught full-time at the school — it would have taken them
many weeks to get the job done.

As a citizen of South Korea, Jin Seop had done his required
service in the South Korean army. As a soldier he was responsible for managing computing facilities. He had experience
installing network computers and building labs. And I had
recently assisted a non-profit organization in Pittsburgh in making plans to set up and operate computer labs in low-income
neighborhoods. So we were both familiar with the process. And
there was a pressing need for more computers at ASYV. So Mike,
Ilan, Jin Seop and I agreed that helping build additional computer labs would be one of our consulting tasks.

We talked to Ilan and persuaded him to allow some students to
assist us in setting up the computer labs. We recommended a few
students we had met during our first week at ASYV. These students
were enthusiastic about computers and anything related to technology. They were inquisitive. Whenever they had free time, they
approached us and asked questions about how computers work and
how their parts were interconnected. Two students, Emmanuel and
Justin, were really enthusiastic. They were either sixteen or seventeen years old and lived in the same residential house. It was their
third year at ASYV. They were taking IT courses at Liquidnet High
School, and they were both at the top of their classes.

We also thought ASYV should have a student-led IT club.
We took on structuring and organizing a formal IT club as
another consulting task. We wanted the IT club to be integral to
the management and maintenance of technology at ASYV. We

thought that, in the long term, the students and ASYV would benefit from the IT club. ASYV was still growing. The technology infrastructure was expanding. Mike was the only person responsible for managing and maintaining it, and he would return to the United States in six months. And we also needed help installing more computer labs.

Jin Seop and I thought that the IT club could help with infrastructure expansion and also help ASYV's technology infrastructure become sustainable. The mission of the club would be to manage and maintain the labs and also provide technical support to the staff. This would create a win-win situation. By maintaining computers and providing support, students would have the opportunity to learn more because they would have to diagnose all types of technology-related problems and find solutions. They would gain practical experience. And ASYV would not need to depend on just one IT volunteer. Emmanuel and Justin became two of the most dedicated members of the newly formed club.

I often worked with members of the new IT club.

Throughout the remaining weeks, Jin Seop and I collaborated closely with Mike in planning, designing and building the computer labs. In each phase, we involved the IT club as much as possible. By the end of our project, we had added two new labs — one in the high school and another in the learning center located in the residential area. And, by working with us, most students in the club had learned how to set up computers and connect them to a network without any help. A few bright members of the club, including Emmanuel and Justin, were becoming ASYV's very own "geek squad" as they developed confidence in their abilities.

We did not use all the donated computers in the new labs. There were still a few dozen computers for ASYV to use for other purposes. It was even suggested that some of the remaining computers would be placed in the residential houses for the students to use. And, if this were to happen, the IT club had the skills to successfully carry out the task.

⊕

At ASYV netbooks were the most popular type of computers used by the teachers and the staff members. Netbooks are portable computers — smaller and lighter than the typical laptops — that had come out within the previous six years. Because of their smaller size, they had less processing power than the typical laptops. In the United States, they gained some popularity when they were first introduced. They were inexpensive and had built-in Wi-Fi capability so they could easily connect to the internet. The average price for a netbook was around three hundred fifty US dollars. But they later were eclipsed by tablet computers like the iPad. As the sales of tablets surged, sales of netbooks declined.

Almost all the teachers and staff members had netbooks and used them for work and to browse the Internet, check email, watch movies, and listen to music. Because of their low processing power, most of the netbooks eventually become overloaded, especially when there are too many movies and music files stored on their hard drives. We noticed a significant slowdown in the netbooks' speed.

Within our first couple weeks at ASYV, teachers and staff members regularly requested our help troubleshooting netbook-related issues. This happened almost two hundred times. Jin Seop and I realized that it would help teachers and staff members for us to give some presentations and a workshop. Topics included the basic functions of the Microsoft Windows operating system and Microsoft Office applications such as Word and Excel, connecting to the Internet via Wi-Fi, utilizing the network drives, and safely surfing the web in order to avoid computer viruses. Other threats were Nigerian email scams in which the sender, who claims to be from Nigeria, requests the recipient's bank account information for use in illegal activities.

The presentations and workshops really helped. There was a great turnout for the workshops, and we soon noticed results. We also distributed some tutorials that we had created. We hoped that the tutorials, along with the presentation slides, would be used by teachers and staff as references.

Rwanda has been installing a fiber optic network throughout the country as part of their development strategy to support Paul Kagame's vision of Rwanda as the "tech hub" of East Africa. The fiber optic network is connected to a submarine cable that runs along the coast of East Africa and provides fast broadband connections.

But the network had not yet reached Nunga. So ASYV, just like many other organizations in Sub-Saharan Africa, still relied on satellite, using small VSAT terminals for Internet connectivity. ASYV's single two-way satellite connection handled all Internet data moving in or out the Village. The VSAT terminal was mounted on the rooftop of Liquidnet High School, the highest point in the village. With this satellite connection serving as a backbone, a wireless local area network (WLAN) was deployed throughout the village to provide Internet access to all Wi-Fi capable devices.

The WLAN infrastructure was the most cost-effective option for Internet distribution. But coverage was inadequate to support ASYV's rapid expansion. New houses were being built, and the number of netbook users was increasing. So there was a need for a new wireless network plan in order to improve the signal coverage. Designing this new wireless network became another consulting task for us. And this time we learned something new.

Aside from setting up our home wireless network routers in our apartments in Pittsburgh or for our parents in their homes, Jin Seop and I were clueless about wireless networks. Most wireless network routers were easy to set up and do not require any knowledge of radio. But designing a large wireless network for a school and a residential area required an understanding of the fundamentals of radio waves. And, by chance, Dr. Alex Hills, who was our advisor for the consulting project with ASYV, was also the "father" of Wireless Andrew, the first campus-wide Wi-Fi network.

Under the leadership of Dr. Hills, a group of engineers and researchers at Carnegie Mellon University had successfully created that network in 1994. Years before Wi-Fi became popular and available to others, Dr. Hills' team built the network, installing cutting-edge access points across the campus. And these access points provided wireless network connectivity — both inside and outside the buildings — to any user with a mobile computer. The Carnegie Mellon network had been carefully designed and implemented.

Almost seventeen years later, Jin Seop and I were trying to replicate, on a smaller scale, that same kind of careful design to improve wireless connectivity for users of mobile computers on a school campus — this time in rural Rwanda.

During our third week, Dr. Hills visited us at ASYV for three days. He came primarily to check on the status of the project and to meet with Ilan, the ASYV Director. But he also gave us a one-day crash course to teach us about radio waves. It wasn't a sit-down course. We walked around the residential area to survey the environment because, as we would learn, radio waves travel and react to their environment.

Jin Seop and I measured Wi-Fi signal coverage
all across the ASYV campus.

Dr. Hills explained to us some of the complexities of radio frequencies. He told us how radio waves carry information and propagate through the environment, and he went over the mathematics needed in order to understand the logarithmic relationship between watts and decibels. This "just-in-time" training gave us an understanding of some of the important attributes of radio waves and the knowledge needed to collect useful data that would guide the new wireless design.

The Android phone that I had brought from the U.S. became our most valuable tool for assessing the wireless signal coverage at ASYV. A free app that I had downloaded turned my phone into a Wi-Fi analyzer. It allowed us to scan the different channels, see some of the settings of the access points surrounding us, and, most importantly, measure the strength of their signals. We visited most of the buildings at ASYV, especially those that were still under construction, to identify the physical obstacles — such as walls and ceilings — that would impair the Wi-Fi signals. We also measured attenuation to determine how much power the Wi-Fi waves would lose as they traveled through the walls of buildings.

It was a thorough assessment, and we eventually used the information we collected to develop a new wireless network plan. We presented the plan to Ilan and Mike, and we discussed our findings in detail with them. At the last meeting before our departure, it was agreed that Mike would implement the new design.

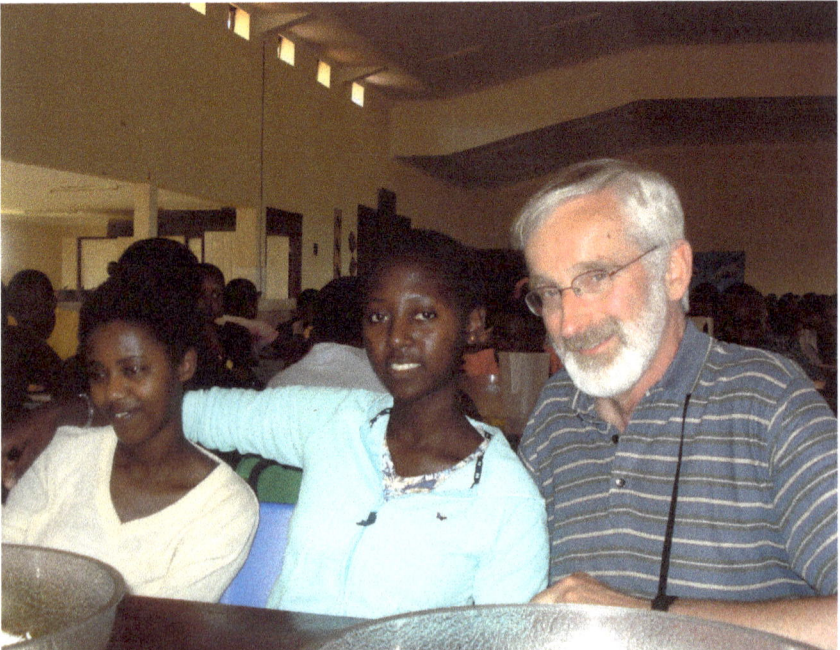

Two ASYV students had lunch with Dr. Hills.

My time in Rwanda was one of the best experiences in my life. After I returned to Pittsburgh, the experience pushed me to reflect on my life. It happened at a decisive time. I only had one more semester left before I was to finish my graduate studies and start my professional career. As a result, I was able to reevaluate and redefine both my professional and personal objectives in life.

At the end of the first semester of my senior year in high school, I had made the decision to attend Morehouse College for my undergraduate studies. My decision was based on many factors, but what influenced me most at the time were the many civil rights activists who were graduates of the small liberal arts college in Atlanta, Georgia. One notable alumnus was the late Dr. Martin Luther King. Former students, such as Dr. King, had the courage to risk their lives and speak against the injustice that was happening daily in their society. The actions they took and the sacrifice they made in the face of seemingly insurmountable adversity required great leadership — and many of those leadership traits were developed at Morehouse College.

I wanted to develop the same leadership skills — skills I believed would be useful to have in a developing country like the Republic of Guinea, a country that was still struggling politically and facing societal difficulties that seemed insurmountable. That was my personal goal, and my liberal arts education at Morehouse helped me develop some of the needed skills. But, in my last year at the college, I unintentionally lost sight of that goal. I don't know how it happened. Perhaps I was focused on other things.

The ten weeks I spent in Rwanda helped me to regain that passion. In a way Rwanda is similar to Guinea. Living in Rwanda for almost three months, I saw a political and economic atmosphere comparable to Guinea. I noticed a need for better leadership. I'm not saying that there is a complete lack of leadership, but it doesn't seem to be present where it is most needed, at the bottom of the pyramid.

I also discovered a new passion. I realized that teaching brings me satisfaction. Once a week in the afternoon, I taught web development concepts and technologies to any member of the IT club at ASYV who was interested in learning. I enjoyed sharing my knowledge. The students' enthusiasm and reaction when they grasped the new material really motivated me. I knew I was making a positive difference. And, since making a positive difference is a source of happiness for me, I hope to be teaching, on a part-time basis, sometime in the near future.

I don't take for granted the opportunities I've had in life. I consider myself very fortunate. I benefited from my family, and I am very grateful for the values and culture they passed on to me. I'm also aware of the fact that many people of my age with the same country or continent of origin will never have the same opportunities. So I think that someone like me, privileged to attend some of the best schools in the United States, has an obligation to contribute to the political, social and economic improvement of developing countries in Africa.

Even though I'm still looking for my real purpose in life, I can say that my experience as a student consultant in Rwanda steered me closer to the answer.

CHAPTER FOUR

GHANA 2008

KATHRYN (KAYT) DICKENS

I was ten when our family dog Pasha died. Being our parents' first baby, she was older than my sister and me, and she had a long and beautiful life — especially when we treated her as our doll and dressed her up before going for walks. Now that I'm adult, I love imagining two little girls and a dog dressed in a man's work shirt and pants, out for a casual walk. But her death was the first tragic event of my life, and I cried for many nights.

After a few weeks of mourning, I started asking my parents when we could get a puppy. They had established a party line, and they stuck to it. "No way — you're going to college in a few years and guess who'll be stuck with the dog?" How does a kid argue with that?

But, where there's a will, there's always a way. I don't remember how I found out about Guide Dogs for the Blind, based in San Rafael, California. The organization breeds and trains dogs, which are then paired with blind people as their seeing eyes. In other words, blind people are given a friend who is trained to see for them. I'm sure you've seen a dog deftly guiding someone, crossing a street, taking public transport, boarding an airplane, or going to work.

Well, who trains these wonderful creatures? First a "puppy-raiser," and then a professional. Guide Dogs for the Blind spares nothing in carrying out their mission. They say that each dog that graduates and serves a blind person is worth around 10,000 dollars. The dogs are trained by professionals for six months, but only half of them pass the course. Others have a "career change," which means they fail the program but become normal family pets. There can be many reasons. Examples are: health screenings that indicate bad hips, unruly behavior at inappropriate times, and chasing after balls or birds.

Guide Dogs for the Blind is great at what they do. Testimonials from blind people who have these dogs tell the story. I've chatted with almost every blind person accompanied by a guide dog that I've ever encountered, and they all say that the dogs liberate them and become their best friends.

The dog-human teams are carefully selected for each other so that they'll get along well. Sometimes, during their month of training together at the school, changes are made because temperaments aren't compatible. I attended a couple of graduation ceremonies where each pair, master and companion, who'd trained together in San Rafael for one month, walked across the stage, accepted their diplomas and began their lives together. There were smiles and tears of joy — and also some sobbing children who had lost their dogs to a higher cause. Alumni and families gathered to celebrate. It was powerful stuff.

I was determined to bring another dog into our family, and I had an airtight presentation. We wouldn't have a dog for more than two years at a time, and I would be training the dog for a noble purpose!

I knew I had to have all the answers ready before I made the pitch to my parents. "No weak links. I must convince them," I thought.

It was pre-Internet, and I started gathering information. I found that guide dog puppy raisers were normal people — just like me and my family. I also learned that there were commitments. Join your local 4-H club to connect with the other puppy raisers in your area, attend weekly dog-training classes, puppy-proof your house and life, and then you get a puppy. The catch? You had to give the puppy back when it was about two years old and perfectly trained. Then it received six intense months of training and then "graduated" to become a guide dog!

I was convinced this was the perfect solution. And it was! They said yes! On the condition that this dog was my responsibility and no one else's. I would pick up its poop, feed it, and be the sole trainer. My parents would be the tolerant, supportive, and generally awesome people that they already were. And they would drive me to meetings because I was a mere twelve years old! After a home-inspection and interview by the guide dog school, and a three month wait, I got a call one day to come and pick up my puppy.

The Guide Dogs for the Blind campus in San Rafael is one of the most beautiful communities I've ever seen. And it's a dog lovers' heaven! The place is situated among oak trees, and it's a micro version of a typical American community, with crosswalks, traffic signals, houses, and offices. There are dogs everywhere — dogs being trained by professionals, dogs and their blind masters who've returned for refresher courses and staying in one of the cottages on campus, and dogs who are sick or injured that are back for some R and R.

The puppy kennel is heaven on earth. Row after row of kennels with gorgeous German shepherd, Labrador retriever, and golden retriever puppies, all less than twelve weeks old! They are released into several yards for play time several times a day. Every time I visited the campus, I allowed at least half an hour to plop down in the middle of one of the yards and lie back to absorb the energy and enthusiasm of puppies romping and playing, chewing on my shirt, and tugging my hair.

I still cherish the pictures of the day I went to pick up my first puppy. I had braces. I was awkward and super-dorky (come on, it was the mid-90s), but my smile was as wide as the camera frame. Hirsch, an adorable 12 week old white Labrador retriever, was the cutest puppy ever. And he was mine!

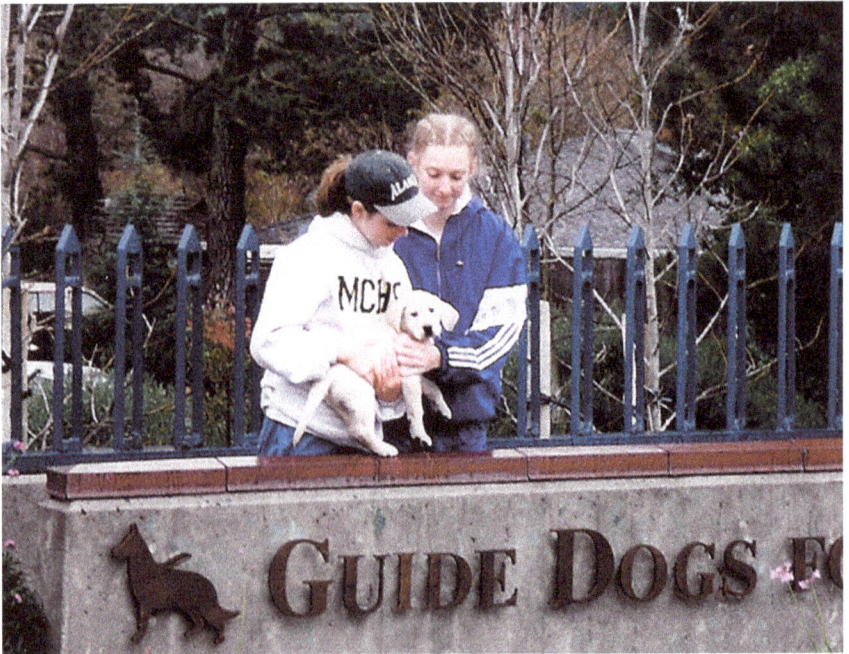

I met my new puppy Hirsch for the first time at Guide Dogs for the Blind.

I enjoyed the puppy training classes — I learned a lot too. There were strict instructions for raising these dogs: feeding them out of their bowls and never by hand, teaching them to "do their business" on command, always letting them sleep in the trainer's room but never in the bed, and never, ever letting the puppies play with a ball. You can imagine that it's a challenge to keep a retriever happy without a ball.

Hirsch grew to be gigantic — not fat but a big, strong dog. He was an alpha male who listened only to me — and only when he wanted to. He liked to hump people, and this mortified a young teenager like me. I'll never forget the day I had my new freshman friends over to my house for the first time. This was my chance to be cool and show off my awesome house and dog.

Hirsch was a little over a year old and fully grown. He loved people and had rushed up to my friends. He was a shoulder-bumping, tail wagging, white storm. He was very excited to meet my friends, and most of them thought he was cool. When the initial love had worn off, we went to the kitchen to get some ice cream. But one kid hung back, and, when I looked over, this is the scene that was unfolding:

Hirsch had picked the class clown, Cranor — that was his last name — as his victim. He had jumped up to put both of his paws on Cranor's shoulders, and, before I could stop him, Hirsch was humping Cranor. Everyone stared in horror. Cranor didn't have a dog and didn't like dogs. He froze. He did not move because he didn't know what to do, and he was scared of this gigantic dog! I screamed at Hirsch, who looked at me and continued, disregarding my authority. When I was inches away from grabbing his collar, he dismounted and ran off.

Hirsch was good fun and a beautiful creature, but I wasn't heartbroken (and neither were my parents) when he was called into service at a year and a half old. We were told that he had been selected to offer his talents as a "breeder." The gods had smiled upon him.

After the Hirsch experience, my mother had strong opinions about the breed and sex of our next puppy. So, with three years left before college, I called Guide Dogs for the Blind and said that I would love to raise another one, as long as it was a golden retriever and female!

Sure enough, in six months I got a call to come and pick up my puppy. My grandparents were visiting from Iowa, so the whole family piled into our minivan, and we made a day trip of it. I practically ran into the kennel to see who would be my next dog. Each litter of puppies at Guide Dogs for the Blind is born to dogs that have been selected as breeders, and the school names each litter in alphabetical order. Each time a female has a litter of puppies, her human family is tasked with naming all of the babies in the litter using a single letter of the alphabet. For example, my first puppy Hirsch was part of an "H" litter.

The kennel keeper at the front desk asked my name and then grabbed the bag of supplies for my puppy — the bags are labeled with the puppy's name. But the top of the bag read "Basket". The other bags said things like "Bailey" or "Buckley," cute names that I liked. But what was this "Basket" business? I started to shake my head, and my lower lip began to tremble and tears began to well. But by this time Grandma, Grandpa, Dad, Mom, and my sister were crowded around me. I looked at the man helplessly and squeaked, "Can I trade for one of the other names?" Seriously. Who wants to stand at the park yelling "Basket! Basket! Come!"

Basket was the pick of the litter — beautiful, smart, and fun to be around. Trainers argued over who could take her home for the weekend whenever we left her in the kennel during trips. And she is still one of the smartest dogs I've ever known. But she was the one who had a 'career change' and didn't become a working guide dog. I would be lying if I said I didn't scream and jump up and down with joy when the Guide Dog school called to tell me she could stay with our family.

The official record reported that she was stellar for four months of her professional training, and then, when they put the harness on her, she simply would not stop eating food and trash off the ground or chasing birds! These are still her biggest weaknesses. Well, also making things disappear from the kitchen counter. Whole loaves of bread, blocks of cheese, chocolate cakes, etc. She has made people think they were losing their minds because of her sly thievery. But she's not a good liar. Just when you're thinking "No, seriously, didn't I leave that sandwich right here?" and gazing around the room in wonder, you catch a glimpse of her over near the corner, head between her paws, pleading with those big beautiful brown eyes saying "I have something to tell you, please don't be mad."

Soon I went off to college, but Basket still lives with my mother. She's an old, old dog, but she still "does her business" on command, and remembers all of her training. The best part for Basket? The day her career changed she had her first encounter with a tennis ball, and that dog hasn't had less than two in her mouth at a time since then!

⊕

For a few summers during my childhood I volunteered on service projects organized by the United Methodist Church. These were week-long adventures with other teens ranging in age from 12 to 18, supervised by adult volunteers and conducted in partnership with local social welfare organizations. I participated during two summers on three different projects. Two were on a Paiute reservation near Pyramid Lake in Nevada, and the third was in the Appalachian Mountains in Tennessee. But the Indian reservations weren't as idyllic as I'd imagined.

I was a "roofing specialist." I cut my teeth on the roof of a mobile home in the Nevada desert, where I spent eight hours a day for seven straight days re-roofing the trailer. We were in a town of about 1,000 people, and we stayed in the high school gym. Each night we had a cultural exchange, usually elders sharing their tribe's stories with us. I loved those nights. The material poverty but cultural wealth of Native Americans impressed me.

The second summer I was with my cousins on a project in the Appalachian Mountains. I felt extra-special because I was the only participant who wasn't from the First United Methodist Church of Ames, Iowa. My grandmother had sponsored this trip for my cousins and me. So I packed up and flew to Iowa, where I joined the group for our road trip to Tennessee. I was excited to visit a new part of the country, and I was really excited to spend time with my cousins and their friends.

I hadn't known that a place so rural, underdeveloped, and impoverished existed in the United States. The house was in the middle of a tiny clearing in an Appalachian forest. It looked like someone had logged the spot and then burned the debris. The house was a tiny mobile home trailer, and the first truly "off-grid" home I'd ever seen. The house had a tiny generator that only ran for a short time each day. And there was no running water. The non-flush toilet shared by the five household members, drained solid and liquid waste into a pipe that emerged from the back of the trailer. The pipe ended five feet from the exterior wall, draining into an open sewage ditch that ran along the back of the trailer. We were told it would be best to "hold it." But, if we had to use the toilet, we were required to ask for water to toss in afterwards. And this was in America!

So I again found myself on a roof. This time we had to rip off the old shingles first. So we began by stomping around to find the main structural beams. All of a sudden we heard a cracking sound, and Andy, my younger cousin, gasped. He had put his foot through the old rotted roof, and this is what we saw: Great Grandma was lying on a hospital bed in the middle of the living room, with an IV in her arm and an oxygen mask over her face, staring up at us. I thought, "Thank God she's wearing that mask." Why? Because the hole around Andy's leg revealed dead rat and snake carcasses and other rotting organic material.

This happened when I was 14. I'm almost 30 years old now, but I still remember it because it shocked me in two ways. One shock was the poverty that existed in the US. ("Aren't sub-Saharan Africans and sub-continental Indians the only people who live like this?" I wondered.) And the other shock was that health care for poor people can be so bad! It broke my heart to see somebody's great-grandmother living her last days like that.

⊕

I graduated from the University of California Davis with a BA in International Relations, and one thing was clear to me. I wanted to volunteer with the United States Peace Corps. I applied, and I was offered a chance to be an IT teacher-trainer in Cameroon. Sub-Saharan Africa was definitely not my ideal location, but I wasn't offered a choice. I was invited to serve in a country that the Peace Corps chose. Take it or leave it. I took it. And I'm glad I did.

Cameroon is a country of many ethnicities and languages — 265 languages, to be exact. The country is roughly the size of California, with a population around 20 million. There are ten provinces, and the seven in the tropical south are more densely populated than the three Sahelian provinces of the Grand North. Northern Cameroon looks like the pictures you see of Mali and Chad: desert-like conditions, a long and very hot dry season, subsistence farming often thwarted by drought, and mostly Muslim people. The south looks like the pictures you might see of Nigeria and Equatorial Guinea: humid tropical rainforests, red dirt, year-round rain providing luscious fruits and vegetables, lots of pork and beef, lots of beer drinking, and mostly Christian people.

Cameroon is officially a bilingual country — French and English — but only two provinces really speak English. They are the south and southwest provinces that border Nigeria. You would have a hard time navigating the country if you didn't speak some French. French and English are, for Cameroonians, second, third or sometimes fourth languages, after a local dialect that depends on ones village.

I spent three months training with my fellow IT workers in the tropical south, and we each stayed with a different host family. I really bonded with my "brothers and sisters" in my host family, and I found my host father to be a wealth of information and advice. My host mother made sure that Guy, her youngest son and the family member who was the best French speaker, was my household teacher. Guy showed me how to wash my clothes by hand and where to find the water barrel if I wanted to take a bucket bath. Every morning Guy prepared my coffee and a sardine juice omelet over an open fire. He was my best friend for a while.

As my French improved, Guy's siblings started hanging out with me more, and the girls fought over who would braid my hair. It really hurt so I only let them do it once. But I spent many hours in the "kitchen" with them. The kitchen was really the entire courtyard. It had a room with a fire for cooking, and the rest of the space was used for things like shucking corn and peeling veggies. I really loved evenings and weekends, when two or three of the kids would invite me to walk with them through the fields and among the hilltops where other families lived. These people farmed areas of forest that had been cleared years before, but it still seemed like a jungle as I walked among ferns twice as tall as me and gigantic trees rising hundreds of feet. I listened to strange bird and monkey chirps. It was fantastic.

When my training was complete, I said goodbye to my family and fellow volunteers and boarded a train to start my trip

north. Traveling only 300 miles in Cameroon was an epic journey. It required an 18-hour train ride and another eight hours on
a large, antique Greyhound-type bus. At the end of the road I
arrived in my new hometown, Maroua, the capital of the
Extreme North Province.

I was the only volunteer in the entire province to have both
running water and electricity — at least most of the time. My
town had a population of about 200,000. And Maroua is a "destination" in Cameroon. It is the only place from whence you can
do a "safari," and Cameroonians really like the calm and quiet of
this sleepy and dusty town that is so different from the tropical
south. Several international NGOs have offices in Maroua, and
there are Internet cafes, three international banks, and two hotels
with air-conditioning and swimming pools. It is quintessential
sub-Saharan Africa, but it's not really village life. Nevertheless, it
suited me well. To teach IT you do need electricity and an Internet connection — at least once in a while.

Most of the people of Maroua are Muslim. But the community's religious tolerance was striking. Christians were included in
the Muslim holidays. They were invited to celebrate and dine
with Muslims on their holy days. And Muslim feasts and parties
last for days. The post-Ramadan party and *Fete de Moutton* were
week-long celebrations filled with visiting and eating at the home
of every friend and colleague. Weddings were similar except that
you stay at the house of the bride's family all week — to help out
and to eat.

In Maroua I was often sick with amoebas, little creatures living in my intestines and causing me much discomfort on a daily
basis. Usually one contracts amoebas from ingesting something
that has human feces on it. I was sure it was from the vegetables
I was eating raw and the occasional salad I ate at a favorite dive
bar. And yet I never stopped eating them, so I guess I have myself
to blame for the continual discomfort. I contracted malaria one

time, and that was ugly, but it wasn't as bad as when my mother had amoebas and malaria at the same time when she visited me.

Illness is a serious problem in the developing world. Work and education time are lost when children and adults are afflicted with diseases that have been eradicated in developed countries. It's important to treat such maladies immediately to prevent a worsening of the symptoms.

My friend Kelly, who lived in Tokemberi, a rural village about an hour away from Maroua, called one day to ask that I come to spend a night to help her. I agreed without knowing what she needed "help" with. I arrived in Tokemberi to find Rachel, another volunteer, and Kelly hovering over a book titled "Where There is No Doctor." This book is famous among Peace Corps volunteers. It details everything from how to combine over-the-counter drugs to combat malaria when no doctor is available, to how to conduct minor surgeries on yourself, to treating intestinal worms. I have a weak stomach with all things medical, and, when I saw these two ladies hovering over this particular book, red flags went up.

It turned out that Kelly, who had recently returned from a few weeks in the tropical south of Cameroon, had contracted a mango fly. Mango flies are nasty little buggers. They lay their eggs in laundry that's drying outside on a line. Then, when you put on your shirt, the larvae find a nice open pore in your skin, wiggle in, and incubate. Eventually you wonder what hurts on your back, you look in a mirror and see a gigantic pimple that, of course, you try to pop. But you cannot pop this pimple that just keeps becoming bigger and redder. When it hurts like mad, you realize that you have a mango-fly infection.

I realized that my task was to help remove this insect from Kelly's back. My knees went weak and my stomach flipped. I think I made a gagging sound, too.

But, fortunately, Rachel derives joy from all things gross, so for her this was going to be fun. She had determined from the helpful "Where There is No Doctor" that we were going to suffocate the worm by covering the entire pimple with Vaseline. He would be forced to wiggle to the surface to get air, and we would grab his head with the tweezers and yank him out. Seriously!

I volunteered to not watch any of it — instead I would hold Kelly's hand. We all took our places, and Rachel spread on the Vaseline. Then the electricity went out. So we took a couple of minutes to find candles and light them. When we could see again, the little bugger had emerged! Rachel, cool as a cucumber, grabbed the sucker with the tweezers and pulled him out while Kelly groaned and I screamed. And probably gagged again, too.

Who could forget this experience? As volunteers in a remote part of a developing country, in a village without a doctor, we learned how to deal with things all by ourselves. Kelly contracted something that didn't even exist in America, and we figured out how to get a worm out of her back with just a book and friends to help. You don't learn this stuff in school. Even today I'm grateful that it wasn't me with the mango fly in my back.

I finished my Peace Corps service without many other gross experiences. But my social and professional experiences were mind-bending. Volunteering in Cameroon was one of the best experiences in my life because of the learning and growth that were packed into a two-year period. I was challenged on all fronts, and there was no retreat into comfort. But the beauty of the experience was that I could make it whatever I wanted it to be. There were rules and bureaucracy to navigate, but Peace Corps gives you a chance to do something important. And it's not pushing papers around in a file cabinet.

For me, life in Peace Corps was a mixture of triumph and failure. There were days when I wasn't sure I could go on, and there were days when I didn't want to go home — ever. But the latter seemed to outnumber the former. And, like other Peace Corps volunteers, I have some hilarious, disgusting, funny, scary, and incredible stories.

⊕

I arrived at Carnegie Mellon University just six months after I was sent home from Peace Corps, for not wearing a bicycle helmet. (That's another story.) I was still mentally in transition from my time in stark, dry, insufferably hot, Muslim-dominated Sahelian Africa to the U.S.

I needed to get out of my parents' house and move on with my life. But I also needed to get a graduate degree, and fast, to be competitive in the job market. So I chose Carnegie Mellon from the three schools that had accepted me because its program was only one year long. And the program started only two months from my acceptance. It started in May.

I was excited to be on to my next adventure, but I hadn't realized that graduate school would be far different from my undergrad experience. I wouldn't be able to freely choose from an array of interesting classes. I was enrolled in a one-year MS program in Public Policy and Management, and my classes were pretty much prescribed. Obvious. Right? Well, it hadn't been obvious to *me*, so I found myself miserable and stressed out most of the time.

But, halfway through my Carnegie Mellon year, I discovered Joe Mertz and his interest in "technology for development." Before I met Joe, I thought that Carnegie Mellon wasn't the right place for me. I was surrounded by people who wanted to work for the federal government or become management consultants with big consulting firms. I wanted to understand policy creation, but I also wanted to get back into the international sphere — pronto! I hoped that the second part of my Public Policy and Management degree program would be useful in international development work. The jury is still out on that one.

But Carnegie Mellon became a new and brighter place for me when I met Joe. I found a course I could get into. Called "Technology for Development," it was taught by Joe and a small team of professors who were technologists with a global perspective. They had some interesting projects. I took the class, a seminar examining technology in global development, and then I asked Joe to mentor my graduate student team consulting project.

My project team and I worked for the United Nations Development Program (UNDP) Equator Initiative. We created an online portal to connect prior and future recipients of the prestigious UNDP Equator Initiative Prize. One member of the team was Phillip, who would later become my husband. We traveled together to Guatemala and Belize to interview some of the nongovernmental organizations that had won the prizes. We conducted needs assessments in person and via Skype. Then we corresponded with partners in Africa and Asia via email. Joe was a fantastic mentor, and he guided our project to a successful conclusion.

Then one day Joe encouraged me to apply to work on a consulting project in Ghana. He said I could become a volunteer consultant in the Technology Consulting in the Global Community (TCinGC) program. I was thrilled to be selected for a consultancy in West Africa. I would be one of the first two Carnegie Mellon students to work for TCinGC in Africa. I couldn't believe my good luck! This had been exactly the kind of work I wanted to pursue in graduate school.

⊕

I met Adrienne White, my fellow consultant, on the plane — in Amsterdam. I hadn't seen her in the airport, and I thought she must have missed the flight. But, when I neared my seat on the plane, there she was, sitting there and smiling. Like me, she was a recent Carnegie Mellon graduate. She had earned a MS degree in network security at the university's Information Networking

Institute. We greeted each other and then fell asleep for the eight hour flight to Ghana.

We were met at the Accra airport by Peter, a driver from Ashesi University, who took us to the home of Suzanne, an American-born professor at Ashesi and a former Peace Corps volunteer who had served in Swaziland. She and her family gave us a warm welcome and some information about Ghana's capital city of Accra as we ate dinner together. And Suzanne gave me a toothbrush (oh, the things I forget when I travel!) before sending us with Peter to our home for the next three months. We were pleasantly surprised to find a furnished apartment in a building owned by Ashesi. It had three bedrooms, two bathrooms with tubs and showers, a tiled balcony, a refrigerator taller than I, and some furniture. To this former Peace Corps volunteer, it looked like luxury!

Adrienne and I posed for a photo shortly after our arrival in Ghana.

We were fortunate to have the mentorship of Dr. Alex Hills. Dr. Hills was Joe's partner in Technology Consulting in the Global Community, and every summer one of them would visit each team of Carnegie Mellon consultants working in a developing nation. We had been in Accra for about a week when Dr. Hills showed up with his consulting wisdom, lessons, advice, and some money to treat us to things we couldn't afford. We both were appreciative!

We had sit-down strategy sessions, where, in a very short time, Dr. Hills taught Adrienne and me the consulting model and framework we would need for our project. With his guidance we were able to use our time efficiently to deliver the results that Ashesi University needed.

One of my favorite days in Accra was when Dr. Hills rented a car with a driver, Eric, who took us all around town, pointing out restaurants, museums, theaters, shopping centers, and beaches. We stopped at a museum with beautiful local art and cultural relics from throughout Ghana's history. This was the first time I actually saw the chains and armor that were used in the slave trade. Images of Africans being rounded up and sold from the Ghana's "Gold Coast" were powerful. I learned more in that two-hour museum stop than I would all summer about the history of Ghana's three major tribes, colonialism under the British, and the country's subsequent, hard-earned independence. Ghana was the first African country to gain independence from a colonial power.

⊕

We spent a few days getting acquainted with our new lives and jobs. Our project was to migrate the university's spreadsheet-based class registration and student information system to a student records management system that could be used by faculty, students, and staff. In our first few weeks we conducted a needs analysis and interviewed key stakeholders, from the university president to staff and faculty to second-year students. Then we researched software solutions and spoke with Ghanaian representatives of companies like Oracle and PeopleSoft.

Adrienne and I interviewed an Ashesi staff member.

Finally we selected several candidate products. We set up demonstration versions on computers in a campus lab, and then we asked members of the university community to come and test each one. We recorded their comments and preferences.

Later we whittled the system choices down to two and presented our recommendations to the university executives, who made the product selection decision. We helped them implement their chosen system, "Focus SIS," an open-source product developed by a company in Florida. It was used by high-schools and small colleges in the U.S., and it was perfect for the university's needs. We helped Gyamfi, a computer science teacher who was also the local database manager, to gather and organize the existing student and course data. Then the Focus-SIS staff moved the Ashesi data into the new system. As we wrapped up our work, a company representative was arriving to conduct an on-site software orientation and training for the faculty members who would be responsible for maintaining the system.

Our work endeared us to the Ashesi community. Staff and faculty were excited to have a modern student records management system accessible from their offices, and they were helpful in answering questions, providing information, and considering software options. Soon after we arrived at Ashesi, they welcomed us into their small community. We ate lunches together in the "cantina." Over local dishes of fish or chicken with rice, beans and cooked vegetables, we bonded with them. Even the university's president and founder, former Microsoft executive Patrick Awuah, regularly dined with us at lunch. The cantina was run by a Ghanaian woman who did all the cooking at home in the morning and then transported the food to the university in huge metal pots full of delicious home-made hot lunches and coolers full of cold juices made from locally grown fruit. Lunch was cheap by American standards, two US dollars for a full, healthy meal. The fellowship was priceless.

One of our best experiences of the summer came when we were invited to dine at Dr. Nana Apt's house. An Ashesi professor of sociology, Dr. Apt was the first Ghanaian woman to earn a Ph.D. She spent many years working to achieve equal educational opportunities for Ghanaian girls, especially poor girls. And every summer she managed a girls' camp in Accra for girls from remote and impoverished villages. The week-long girls' camp activities ranged from classroom sessions with math and science experiments to games and confidence-building exercises. The girls stayed in a dormitory and, as I watched them, I remembered my own youthful experiences in overnight camps. At the beginning of the camp, the girls arrived quiet and timid, rarely making eye contact. At the end of the camp, they left with big smiles and fresh confidence.

Adrienne and I idolized Dr. Apt. When she invited us and Carol Asamoah, our project supervisor, to her house for lunch, we were excited. Carol picked us up and took us from the hustle and bustle of Accra to the small, quiet suburb where Dr. Apt lived in a house on a hill. We were greeted by two huge but very friendly "guard" dogs (Rottweiler and Doberman mixes), several cats, and Dr. Apt. She gave us a tour of her house. We were so taken with the fantastic view of the sea and the city that we dined outside on her deck. That afternoon, when Dr. Apt opened her home and her heart to us for a ladies' lunch, was one that I'll never forget. Dr. Apt's kindness of spirit, wisdom, and phenomenal accomplishments rank her as one of my top role models.

Lunch at Dr. Apt's house. Left to right, me, Carol, Dr. Apt, and Adrienne.

Another experience we enjoyed was going to a World Cup playoff game of the Ghana "Black Stars" verses the Gabon "Panthers." Our friend Nana, a fellow Carnegie Mellon student and Ghanaian national, was spending that summer in Accra working at an internship with Women's World Banking. He invited Adrienne and me to the game with his cousins and friends. We met at the gate and knew immediately that we were under-dressed. His group was outfitted with Zulu horns, wild spray-painted hair, Ghana jerseys, scarves, flags, t-shirts, etc. But they loaned us some stuff to spice up our outfits so we could blend in a bit. For me it was a scarf and a horn. Adrienne got a hat.

The seating was first-come, first-served. Nana led the way down to field-level seats, where we staked out our row. These were the best seats I'd ever had at a sporting event! The game was competitive, but the hometown Black Stars won 2-1, and the crowd went wild. We went wild with them, blowing our horns and dancing on the seats. Ghana was going to the World Cup!

Ghana was victorious at the World Cup playoff game.

The streets were packed with people celebrating, and we ended up walking a couple of miles before finding a taxi to take us home. But we didn't mind! Spirits were high, and it was great! Adrienne and I both felt pride at being a part of this community. Our team had won!

⊕

We tried to do at least one excursion per month. One of our first trips was about two hours up the coast, to a castle that was once used in the slave trade. It was one of the most disgusting buildings I've ever seen — but not because it was ugly or crumbling. It was in good condition, well built but with an ugly purpose. The tour guides took us into a dungeon with holding chambers, and I tried to conjure images of thousands of men and women locked into tiny cells without sunlight or sewage systems, treated like animals and then sold like meat.

I was repulsed, but I appreciated the Ghanaian government's effort to tell and retell this history to each new generation so that we would never return to such barbaric treatment of human beings. It was inspiring to see groups of school children taking the same tour, and it was interesting to be with Adrienne, a black American. She was moved by the experience. She told me about her experiences in both Africa and America. It was food for thought. We are about the same age, and we had attended the same graduate school, but our life experiences could not have been more different.

I have never felt so well suited for a position before or since. I felt comfortable in my responsibilities to Ashesi University and to TCinGC. Adrienne and I were a good team. We became close — almost inseparable. We worked all day together, we ate lunch together, we went grocery shopping together, and we ate dinner together.

But soon we both needed some space. After we gained confidence in our new surroundings, we began finding our own paths in Accra. I was drawn to the ocean and beach. But these weren't California beaches. The beaches in Accra were littered with debris like discarded flip-flops and used drug needles. There was, and still is, a big problem with drug trafficking in Ghana. And, as I explored the coastline further, I discovered slums with aluminum-sided and cardboard box houses built haphazardly and extending to the water's edge.

And there was the stench. Coastal Ghanaians are fishing people. They have beautifully painted fishing boats that they take out in the sea each day. They drop their nets in the morning and retrieve their catch in the evening. They're beautiful to watch as they untangle and lay their nets out to dry. Teams of men and women sing and chant while they work. But the fish parts stunk. And, in the humidity, the stink enveloped me.

I watched fishermen work with their nets on the beach.

I came to love two beaches — both maintained by hotels for their guests. On my volunteer salary, anything more than a Fanta orange pop or Strella beer was beyond my budget. So I was "strategic." I took my time and waited to place my order until someone came all the way out on the beach to ask for it. Then I milked that drink for longer than any normal person would spend on three.

When I returned home, all I could talk about was Ghana. The three months at Ashesi were the most rewarding challenge I'd had in the then-recent past. Adrienne and I had worked as professional consultants, and our final work product was exactly what Ashesi needed. I had walked away with a great example of my work. I wanted to continue doing this kind of consulting for the rest of my life.

Such profound experiences influence one's worldview, and I continue to work in the world of "doing good." It's easy to get hooked on this world. And it's even easier to get hooked on the fun of exploring new places. I admit that I've always worked just long enough to have enough money for the next adventure. I stretch out travel budgets by trying to find work along the way. Maybe it's the same for people who get hooked on a salary and a lifestyle of over-consumption. I'm addicted to the new and different. My work in international development has enabled me to experience new cultures and places.

But I still haven't made the transition to working in a private company. I was able to string together consulting stints with non-profits until I landed a permanent job at one. But I was miserable behind a desk, especially when I realized there wasn't even a sliver of a chance that I'd visit the organization's projects in Nepal or India. So I left as soon as I could. But, conveniently, my new husband Phillip had been offered a job overseas!

I moved back to West Africa, this time for Phillip's job as a program manager for the Peace Corps in Cape Verde. He was in charge of 25 Small Enterprise program volunteers. But, after a time, it was announced that Peace Corps Cape Verde would be closing. The country was "graduating" to middle income status, and they said that Cape Verde would no longer need Peace Corps volunteers. But, according to Peace Corps volunteers and staff, and according to my own observations, progress hasn't been evenly distributed across the country's population. Middle income status may still be more an ideal more than a reality. Still, Cape Verde is a model African country. It has 85 per cent literacy, a transparent democracy, the rule of law, a low maternal death rate, a high standard of living, and little corruption.

During my time in Cape Verde I had three goals: to learn Portuguese, to earn a TESOL (Teaching English to Speakers of Other Languages) certificate, and to get a job. Goals two and three were easy. I did get my certification, and, through the English Language Institute of Praia, I taught English courses to professionals at the UN Food & Agriculture Organization and at the US embassy. I also found my way to the University of Cape Verde's English department, where I was offered a job with a nice salary and health benefits.

But the first goal was elusive. I never did master Portuguese. It wasn't entirely my fault, though, because Cape Verdeans don't really speak Portuguese. They speak Kriolu, a mix of Portuguese and local languages whose roots are African. But Cape Verdeans are nice people, and they deciphered my broken Portuguese enough for me to navigate. Still, there was much that I missed because of my limited Portuguese language skills.

After I left Cape Verde, my perspective on the "do-good" industries has changed, but my addiction to the "different" has not. I've realized that I have to find a job at an international company that I can tolerate. I will not work for an evil international giant like Coca-Cola, and I could never work for Shell Oil or

DeBeers diamonds, but I'm sure there's a good company out there. I don't know where Phillip and I will end up next, but it's not likely to be a place we've already lived. And I don't rule out volunteering again!

A few years ago I was offered the chance to join the Board of Directors at Education Fights Aids (EFA) International. This non-profit was founded by a group of former Peace Corps volunteers who had been community health workers in Cameroon. Andrew Koleros, one of the founding members, created a network of HIV+ youth in the Extreme North Province. When he completed his service, he formalized the network and created an NGO to which family and friends could contribute. Six years later, with a volunteer Board of Directors, EFA has become an international NGO with five paid staff in Cameroon, and a network of over 500 HIV+ youth and adults.

Here's how it works: From the regional office in Maroua, Cameroon, EFA's country representative and program manager coordinate a network of twelve groups of youth and adults who receive the technical guidance of the regional office staff but maintain their own village associations. Each village association is responsible for its own leadership and financial management, but the association benefits from training and education sessions offered by the EFA staff and current Peace Corps volunteers. In this way health education reaches even small remote villages. It happens because association members bring health information home by doing public talks in their small communities.

As volunteer board members, we handle all of the fundraising, communications, and legal issues. It's a big job for board members, but it's been a unique experience. Through our uses of new — and usually free — technology tools, we've built an organization that is managed remotely. We conduct board meetings quarterly and coordinate among members in Australia, the East Coast of the United States, Cameroon, Cape Verde, and Rwanda. We manage to work full time professional jobs and, at the same time, volunteer big chunks of time to keep EFA International afloat. But you wouldn't suspect this if you visited the regional office in Cameroon. EFA International has become a highly respected organization, boasting partnerships with the Cameroon Ministry of Health, Peace Corps, President's Emergency Plan for Aids Relief (PEPFAR), the UN Development Program, the US embassy, and local hospitals.

Why do we volunteer so much of our time and energy to EFA International? I guess my answer is that it's an investment with a great return. In only six years the organization has already saved and changed lives. I've seen HIV+ kids and adults who were abandoned by their families and left for dead later gain confidence and capability as they completed training with EFA. They became highly respected for the knowledge that they share. Each of them is living proof that HIV+ status doesn't mean life is over.

I've seen HIV+ mothers give birth to healthy HIV- babies. That is one of the most beautiful outcomes of EFA's programs — a new AIDS free generation. There is also the short term outcome of revenue from a shared enterprise. Several associations have plots of land that they cultivate together and share the profits. Other associations store grain or raise livestock and share the profit — all activities that were made possible through small grants from EFA or through technical training and support offered by EFA.

This is why I volunteer so much time to EFA. I went to Cameroon and visited the regional office and several associations in 2011. I saw that the money we raise each year is really making a difference — an amazing difference! It's great to be a part of that. I think I'll be volunteering for the rest of my life.

I guess you can take the girl out of Peace Corps, but you can't take Peace Corps volunteer out of the girl!

In 2011 I returned to Cameroon to work with the EFA International staff.

CHAPTER FIVE

GHANA 2008

ADRIENNE WHITE

Home for me is rural north Louisiana. One could say it was boring, but I'd say I was pretty lucky. See, I had family — a big one! I grew up with a host of maternal and paternal aunts, uncles, and cousins, and I frequently "spent the night" with all of them. And, not only did I meet all of my grandparents and great-grandparents (except one), I had *real* relationships with them. I was blessed.

My mom, who loved her family, carried me with her whenever she visited her relatives. On one of our overnight visits to see her maternal grandparents, my mom said to me, "uno, dos, tres, cuatro, cinco..." with a smile on her face. I was about five years old, and I didn't know what to make of it. She said it again, "uno, dos, tres, cuatro, cinco..." Then she asked me to repeat it. We said it over and over again. She told me it was Spanish, which she was then studying as a minor in college.

She continued to teach me new words, and I got excited about it every time. After she graduated, we practiced Spanish much less. I soon forgot about it — but only for a while.

Mom and I permanently moved in with her parents, Maw-Maw and Papa, after she and my dad divorced. I was around ten years old. My dad moved to another city about 160 miles to the south, but I talked to him regularly and visited occasionally. Despite the divorce, my mom took great care to involve me with my paternal relatives, often accompanying me to their family outings.

My dad's mother, Grandmother, also took great care to involve me with the family. She would often corral her eight siblings and countless nieces and nephews into attending a "function" at her home or at her father's home. These events usually followed Sunday church and often included a spread of collard greens, black-eyed peas, fried chicken, and much more Southern cuisine. They also meant that we "young people" would have to recite an African-American poem that Grandmother had given us. She was truly proud of her history and culture.

Perhaps one of those "history lessons" sparked my interest in Atlanta's Spelman College, a historically black college exclusively for women. I desperately wanted to attend Spelman, and I did everything I could to get there. That included involving myself with a myriad of high school extracurricular activities, one of which was volunteering at my local public library. The librarian allowed me to volunteer on Saturdays, and I was elated. For my entire four years of high school, I volunteered there each Saturday 8:30 a.m. to 12:00 p.m.

Eventually, my dream of going to Spelman came true. I graduated as high school valedictorian and received enough scholarship money to cover all of my college costs. Praise God!

Spelman was everything I imagined it would be . . . and so much more. It was magical. The thinking was different there, and I liked it. Spelman had a course called "African Diaspora and the World," a two semester course that was required of all students. Another curriculum requirement was the completion of two semesters of a foreign language or international studies.

A foreign language? I thought about it, looked into it, and discovered that Spelman had a Spanish curriculum. *JACKPOT!* I knew what I would choose — it was a no-brainer. I quickly finished the required two semesters, but I didn't want to stop. I took several more Spanish classes and then learned of a short, study abroad opportunity.

I desperately wanted to study abroad, but as a mathematics major, I wasn't confident enough to take any of my major classes in Spanish. Plus, one of my scholarships required me to intern each summer at NASA. The odds were really not in my favor.

This study abroad opportunity is perfect...if only I can arrive at NASA two weeks late. I picked up the phone and tried to work out the details, and NASA was OK with my plan. I applied to the program and was accepted.

In early May 2005 I left for Oaxaca, Mexico, along with 30 other students in the program. Half of the group was from Spelman, and the other half was from Morehouse College, Spelman's all-male counterpart located just across the street in Atlanta.

Each student lived with a different host family, but we all took two Spanish classes together at the *Universidad Autónoma Benito Juárez de Oaxaca*. Classes were dismissed in the middle of the day, when we went home to our "families" and ate a hot meal with them. But then we had to walk back to school in the hot sun for our afternoon classes. My walk was about 20 minutes, and I hated that heat!

There was also time to take in the sights and sounds of the city and surrounding area. Spelman's Professor Langhorst arranged a multi-day cultural excursion for us in which we traveled several hours to a town of very poor black Mexicans. We spoke to the children about college and tried to give them hope for the future. Following our time with the students, we traveled by boat and saw the beautiful, natural side of Mexico, far away from the cities and towns.

Outside of the official field trips, we often hung out as a group. We frequented each other's homes, and we went shopping. My favorite store was Chedraui, which is akin to Walmart. We also watched movies regularly, and we ate the absolute best ice cream I've ever had.

What bothered me, but wasn't part of my experience, was the fact that the water was not drinkable, or potable. Dr. Langhorst and other professors warned us repeatedly not to drink the water. They warned us to not even brush our teeth with it! We had to use bottled water for everything. I convinced myself that potable running water truly was a luxury.

After six weeks we returned to the U.S. I liked my Mexican experience, but I was glad to be home.

✦

That summer my NASA project focused on computer network security, and I was intrigued by the subject. I wasn't quite sure what to do with my math degree, but, after returning to Spelman for my final year, I investigated graduate programs in computer networks and network security.

God always has a plan for things. I saw a hallway flyer about Carnegie Mellon University's (CMU's) Information Networking Institute (INI), which had graduate degree programs in information networking and information security. *JACKPOT — AGAIN!*

But I was apprehensive. The student photo rosters showed there were very few African-Americans. In fact, there were none. There was one student from Nigeria and another from Barbados, but they weren't African-Americans. I had never, in all my years of school, been "the only one." I sought advice from Jamar, the student from Barbados. He told me that the courses were difficult but that his color wasn't really an issue.

Even after being accepted to the program, I was still unsure. I visited the INI open house, and the atmosphere was surprisingly inviting. Dena, the INI director, was present, and she gave me a boost of confidence. I decided to go to CMU.

I arrived in Pittsburgh, Pennsylvania, in mid-August, about one week before classes began. My mother was there to help with my move, but she didn't stay very long. Soon I was there by myself. Most of my classmates were from India, and many of them already knew each other. Being an outsider really started to set in.

Academically, INI required the completion of either of two courses: Embedded Systems or Operating Systems (OS). A prerequisite for the latter was an undergraduate course called Computer Systems. OS, I had been told, was a "beast" and that students hardly made it out alive. I didn't want to take the easy way out by opting for Embedded Systems. Plus, I wanted to give myself some credibility with my classmates. So I signed up for the OS prerequisite, Computer Systems, course number 15-213.

Within a week, our first assignment was due. It was a debugging problem. "Bombs" had been placed within a program, and we had to identify where each bomb was. I failed this assignment — miserably. I continued attending the lectures, though, hoping that I would eventually "get it." One day during a lecture I realized I had no idea what the professor was talking about. There was an hour left in the class, but I just left the room. I wasn't going back.

What am I going to do?! It was only week two of the semester. *How am I going to graduate on time if I drop a prerequisite for a class that I need?*

As God would have it, I saw a hallway poster about a course I could use as an elective. The course was "Technology for Developing Communities" (T4DC). It sounded interesting. I needed to make a decision quick, though, because the add/drop deadline was at hand. I met with the T4DC instructor to get a feel for the course, and she emphasized that I would be joining the course two weeks late. I didn't care. I just couldn't go back to 15-213.

Joining T4DC was the best decision I could have made. The material wasn't just "textbook" science; it was "how do we apply it" science. The four instructors were excited about their topics — microfinance, poverty, the 100 dollar laptop, capacity building, and technology trends — all of which excited me, too. I felt so alive in the class. I looked forward to every session.

One of the sessions told us about opportunities that complemented what we were studying. "Technology Consulting in the Community" (TCinC) was a CMU program that allowed students to work with Pittsburgh non-profit organizations during the semester, helping the organizations solve problems with technology. Another opportunity was "Technology Consulting in the Global Community" (TCinGC). It was similar to TCinC, except that the nonprofits, or "partners," were all over the world, and the consultancies were done during the summer. TCinC sounded ok, but I was *really* excited about TCinGC. *Travel to a foreign country, helping people alleviate a problem by using technology?* I was all over it. But then I returned to reality. There was NO WAY I could do a summer consultancy...I had internship obligations due to scholarship requirements. I gave up that dream — at least for a while.

But I really liked T4DC. Final projects, which were 50 per cent of the course grade, were due at the end of the semester. I chose a topic with which I was very familiar: the water infrastructure problem in Oaxaca, Mexico and how technology might ease the problem.

The water problem in Oaxaca bugged me. I found it odd that people couldn't drink their own water or flush tissue down the toilet. I hadn't realized that the U.S. was one of a few countries where one could actually do those things. *How can technology help solve this problem?* Water potability questions plagued me. *Why didn't Oaxaqueños purify their own water?* If they did it themselves, they wouldn't have to rely on a purified-water delivery service, which would ultimately save them money.

Most purification technologies, I learned, were effective enough to make water safe to drink. They could zap most microscopic biological agents, and BAM, the water was ready for consumption. Some methods were more effective than others, but they all worked. Notably, I found that adding a small amount of household bleach could produce the same results. *What?! So why would one even need those fancy, shmancy methods?*

It turned out that, even though purification methods were effective against biological agents, they had little effect on non-biological agents. This was important to know since almost the entire country of Mexico suffered from old, rusty water pipes. With such infrastructure, it was inevitable that the water would contain rust particles (or lead, or whatever material was used for piping). For *Oaxaqueños*, this meant that, no matter how much bleach they added, their tap water would remain unsafe.

One side of me was satisfied because I finally knew *why* the Oaxaqueños did what they did. But another side of me was saddened that their government, to my knowledge, didn't have any major initiatives underway to improve the infrastructure. Access to clean water, as I had learned in T4DC, was essential to human development, and I found it appalling that the government wasn't trying to improve the people's quality of life.

I completed my written report and submitted it. I held my breath. *A- for the semester...YES!*

⊕

My final year at CMU started in the fall of 2007. As God would have it, I saw a poster for TCinGC, which was now accepting applications. *This is my chance!* I would be graduating in the spring with no internship obligations — I was home free. So I applied...and waited for a response.

Months later, near the middle of the spring 2008 semester, Joe Mertz called me. I was so excited to hear from Joe! He had been one of the four instructors for T4DC. Joe was also the TCinGC director. His call was sure to mean good news. And it did. He was calling to tell me I had been accepted for TCinGC! My consultancy would be in the Philippines working on developing supercomputers. The details were still being worked out, but that didn't matter to me — I was just glad I had been accepted.

The Philippines, eh? I began to warm up to the idea. The Philippines had been a Spanish colony from the late 1500s to late 1800s. I got excited about speaking Spanish again.

About a week later Joe Mertz called me again. He told me the Philippines project hadn't worked out, which had me heartbroken. But he quickly told me that I would be going to Ghana, West Africa instead.

Ghana?! OK??? Despite having a command of African-American culture, I realized I knew very little about *African* culture. I suddenly became nervous. *What if I don't fit in? What if I'm rejected by my African brothers and sisters?*

But I couldn't worry about that. All I knew was that a dream had come true for me, and I had to go with it.

Joe later told me that the Ghana project would be the first one in Africa for TCinGC. He said that the project would revolve around helping an up-and-coming private college, Ashesi University College, better manage its student records — a bit different from developing supercomputers!

The consultancies usually had two students on each project, and my partner would be Kathryn "Kayt" Dickens. Kayt, too, was just finishing a master's program. She would be graduating in a few months with a degree in Public Policy and Management from CMU's Heinz College. She had started her program after completing a two-year Peace Corps stint in Cameroon, West Africa, which I thought was really cool. The more I learned about Kayt, the more I wanted to learn about her, and the more I looked forward to working with her on our project.

While we were in the midst of attending class, studying for finals, preparing for graduation, and moving out of our apartments, Joe imposed several requirements on all of us outgoing consultants. We had to attend a multi-session orientation; obtain visas, passports, immunizations, and international student IDs; begin research on our project; and start communicating with our client organizations.

Our orientation described possible cultural differences that a consultant might encounter. One piece of advice was to always eat when invited. Otherwise, one could offend the host. Concerning visas, TCinGC assistant Sarah asked that we surrender our passports to her so she could send them to embassies in Washington, D.C. and obtain visas on our behalf. She would then deliver them to us. *Surrender my passport?! Are you crazy?!* But I had to do it to get to Ghana.

The orientation sessions also covered the immunizations that were required. There were a lot! I went to the Allegheny County Health Department, which was reminiscent of going to the Department of Motor Vehicles — wait, wait, wait and crying babies everywhere! I spent almost the whole day there, but I walked out with my immunizations…and $300 poorer. For malaria prevention, I opted for a daily, oral prescription. *Another $500?! OUCH!*

While we were still in Pittsburgh, Kayt and I began to research our client's situation. Ashesi University wanted to buy a student records management software product. However, as we were taught in T4DC and as reiterated in the orientation sessions, our duty was to understand the problem by starting at the beginning and not where our client wanted to start. In the meantime, we investigated some student records management system (SRMS) products.

Enter Dr. Alex Hills. Dr. Hills was a professor at Carnegie Mellon and a frequent advisor to Joe concerning TCinGC. Dr. Hills was a genius in the realm of telecommunications and engineering. In fact, he had been the first director of the INI in the 1980s.

Dr. Hills began to advise Kayt and me on our project even before we left Pittsburgh. He had a keen interest in Ashesi and agreed to travel to Ghana to ensure that we started off in the right direction. I would later learn that this was characteristic of Dr. Hills — giving, reaching out, going above and beyond, and taking the first step. He emailed us:

> *Adrienne and Kayt,*
>
> *I think you're both CMU graduates now. Congratulations!*
>
> *I'm looking forward to seeing you both in Accra. If you need to contact me before you leave the US, please use my phone number below.*
>
> *I'm adding at the end of this message a summary of the consulting process steps that were discussed in your TCinGC briefing with Joe Mertz. I'm hoping that you will have made some*

progress on the first two or three of these by the time I arrive in Accra. I'm looking forward to discussing them with you when I arrive.

Hopefully, you'll be able to complete the first six steps in the first two weeks or so of the project. That will leave weeks 3-9 for "implement work plan" and "document outcomes."

I'm looking forward to seeing you in Accra.

Have a good trip

Alex

We subsequently passed emails back and forth, getting to know each other, and I openly expressed my excitement about going to Ghana. He began to share some ideas about how our project could develop, as well as synopses of specific SRMS products that Kayt and I could investigate. He gave us a great head start:

Kayt and Adrienne,

I've now talked with both of you by Skype, and both conversations were very productive. Thanks.

I'm sending the list of SIS products, as promised. Any time you have between now and departure could usefully be spent researching these on the Web. If you have a printer available, I'd suggest printing Web pages that you think are important — doing this kind of surfing from Ghana may be more difficult.

There are two lists. The first is the list of big commercial products, which are primarily student records systems. The second is a list of open source products, which focus more on instructional support (like Blackboard). I suggest looking for student records capability in the open source products.

You may also find other open source products that I'm not aware of.

Feel free to call me at the number below. Remember that in Alaska it's four hours earlier than Pittsburgh.

Congrats on your new MS degrees!

Alex

About 2 days before our departure date, we got our passports back with the visas attached. I breathed a deep sigh of relief. Things were all set.

I departed Washington D.C.'s Dulles Airport headed to Accra, Ghana via Amsterdam on May 25, 2008, around 5:00 pm local time. Kayt took a different flight but would meet me in Amsterdam.

It was my first time flying with KLM, and I was in hog heaven. They had on-board movies and they constantly fed me *real* food (not peanuts)! I ate, watched a movie, tried to sleep, then awoke to flight attendants trying to feed me again. But sleep didn't come to me. I was excited about what was ahead — and nervous. *What if I don't fit in? What if we aren't able to help Ashesi like we want to? What if we don't know enough to help Ashesi? What if we fail?*

I arrived at Amsterdam's Schipol Airport around 7:00 am local time, after the seven and a half hour flight from Dulles airport. I was tired. I wanted to call home, but it was very late at night in the U.S. So I just wandered around the airport. I unrealistically hoped I'd find a Ghanaian newspaper, and I walked into a news shop. There were no publications from Ghana, but I saw something else that caught my eye... the "adult" magazines were open for all to see, and one of the covers displayed nudity. This sure wasn't home!

Kayt and I found each other on our connecting flight to Ghana. We greeted each other, but then it was back to eating, watching movies, and attempting to sleep.

We arrived in Accra at night. *I am in Africa!!!* My feet were finally touching the soil of my ancestors — awesome! I was free and humbled at the same time.

We had to wait a while in the customs line, but not nearly as long as people who hadn't gotten their visas in advance. *Thank you TCinGC!* Then it was off to get our bags. People were pushing and shoving — it was chaotic! Eventually our bags arrived. We were relieved that all of our luggage had made it.

At this point, I *had* to call my family to let them know I had arrived safely. "Hello! Paris is that you," my mom asked, using my nickname. She spoke in an excited but unsure, high-pitched tone. She was not able to make sense of the numbers that had appeared on her caller ID.

"Yes, it's me, Mom. I made it. I'm using someone else's phone so I can't talk. I'll call you again when I can. Tell everyone I made it. Love you."

"Love you, too."

We were told that someone from Ashesi would pick us up from the airport, but that was all we knew. As we walked outside the terminal, we joined a *sea* of people. There was no way we would be able to find this person, a needle in a haystack! So we just waited for the mystery person to find us.

Like a miracle, a man with an "Ashesi" sign appeared. *God is good!* He quickly moved us away from the crowd. We were so relieved. He told us his name was Peter and that he would take us to our hostel.

We were glad to finally arrive at the hostel; we were very tired. Peter introduced us to Suala, who was the hostel overseer. He was near our age and drove a motorcycle. I thought he was cute. He walked us to our apartment, gave us our keys, and bade us goodnight.

We had been assigned a three-bedroom, two-bath apartment on the third floor. It had a living room with sofa and chairs, a dining area, a kitchen, and multiple beds in each bedroom. We also had a walk-out balcony. Since it was dark and there were no streetlights, we couldn't see any of the neighborhood. Nonetheless, I was surprised that our accommodations were almost luxurious.

We didn't bother unpacking. We went to bed almost immediately.

🌐

The next morning, the sun beamed in mercilessly, waking me up. I tried to go back to sleep but couldn't. I quickly realized it would take a while to adjust to the four-hour time difference.

Half awake, I heard Suala enter the apartment. I wondered if that was acceptable in Ghana. He called to us from the hallway, and I yelled from the bedroom that we were still asleep. He yelled that Peter was here to pick us up. *What?! And no one told us yesterday?!* I yelled again that we were asleep. He surrendered, saying he'd tell Peter to come back for us later. With Suala's "wake up call" and the sun not going away, I decided to get up.

As I approached the dining room, I was shocked. I saw someone breaking into our apartment! A young woman was climbing through the dining room window! I hid in the hallway. I was scared to even scream. *Who is she? What did she come for?* All I could do was watch. *Was this normal in Ghana? First Suala entered the apartment, and now this!* I didn't know what to make of it.

I watched the intruder. She went to the empty third bedroom where there was a suitcase that did not belong to us, and she began scrambling through it. Then she went to the kitchen and started scrambling through the pantry! I finally worked up the nerve to approach her.

"Who are you? What are you doing here?" I asked in my most aggressive and stern tone.

She said that she used to live in the apartment and had left some belongings. She seemed scared herself. I empathized with her and wanted to help. But I made it clear that she didn't live there anymore and that she couldn't just climb through our windows.

I hurried her in collecting her things. She attempted to leave through the window, just as she had come, but I stopped her and showed her to the door. After she left, I locked all the doors and windows.

We arrived at the Ashesi's temporary campus later that morning. Carol Asamoah was the first person we met. Carol was the Acting Registrar and Director of Admissions, and she also oversaw Human Resources and Operations. Carol would be our client representative, the primary contact person for our project.

Ashesi's temporary campus was in a residential area of Accra.

I admired Carol. She was African-American and had moved to Ghana after marrying her husband, a native Ghanaian. She handled herself with such poise, and her speaking skills were superb. I wished I could emulate her — she was polished! Carol was also young and beautiful. She reminded me of the U.S. actress Malinda Williams.

This was one of the three buildings that made up Ashesi's temporary campus.

Carol gave us a campus tour and introduced us to the staff, including Patrick Awuah, the president of Ashesi. Carol knocked on Patrick's door, and he invited all three of us to come in. I jokingly whispered to Kayt, "I wish I could just walk into our president's office," remembering how one needed to make an appointment months in advance to see Dr. Tatum at Spelman or Dr. Cohon at CMU.

Patrick was a cool guy. He listened attentively as we told him about our backgrounds. I noticed the book *The Audacity of Hope* on his desk, and it appeared that he was halfway through reading it. I had received the same book as a graduation gift from my sister a week earlier, but I'd only managed to get through the prologue.

"So you're reading *The Audacity of Hope*? I am too," I said.

He responded, "He's a good guy," referring to the book's author, Barack Obama. I immediately remembered seeing another African man in Amsterdam airport carrying that book. There were a lot of people reading it. Carol jumped in and commented that the upcoming U.S. election was not just a U.S. election but that everyone in the world wanted Obama to win. At that moment, I understood what Michelle Obama meant when she said "For the first time in my adult life, I'm proud of my country."

We spent the rest of the day shopping. Food for the apartment and cell phones were our top priorities. Peter said he'd pick us up at 9:00 am to take us to Ashesi. It was 10:00 pm, and the alarm would go off at 6:00 am. That was my busiest day in a long time, and I was beat. I was ready for bed. *Good night!*

⊕

Soon it was the weekend and Dr. Hills arrived! His mission was to ensure that everything would go smoothly during our ten-week project. He and Joe had a good relationship, and Joe trusted any advice he gave. He had so far advised us from Alaska. I was eager to meet him face-to-face.

We met him at his hotel, which was pretty close to Ashesi. We were sitting in the lobby when his six-foot plus frame appeared. *It's him!* We all hugged and chatted only a few moments. He wanted to make the most of his time with us, and he proposed a few excursions for us. The hotel endorsed one local taxi driver, Eric, and Dr. Hills immediately enlisted him as

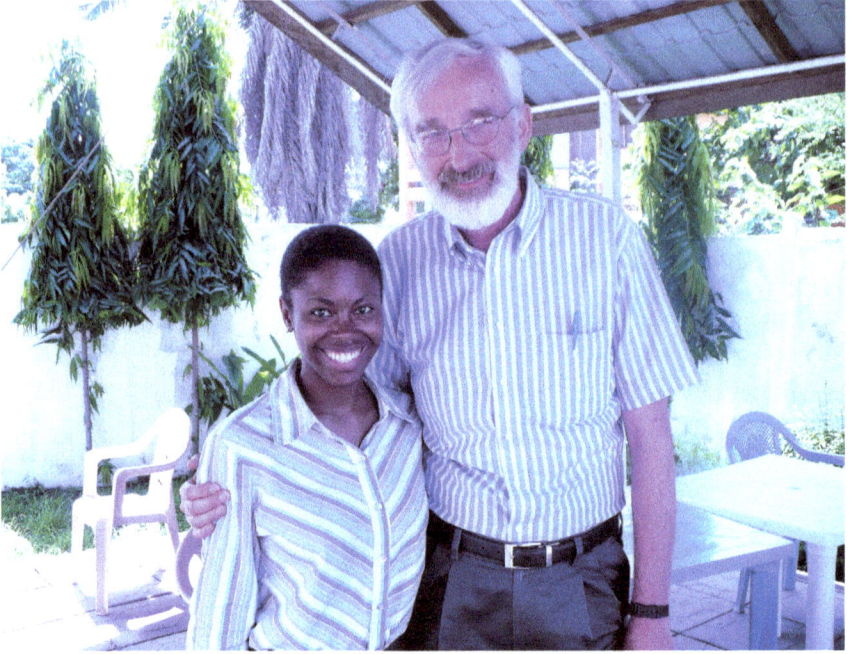

Dr. Hills arrived for a short visit.

our all-day driver and tour guide. Eric's car was small like all the other taxis, but it still stood out. It was pretty hip, especially with its rims.

Off we went. Our first stop was the Labadi Hotel, which was famous for its beach. Eric realized that his car was pretty cramped for Dr. Hills's long legs, and, after he dropped us at the Labadi, he told us he'd be back. He said he would return with his truck. And, boy, was it a truck! It looked like it could go head-to-head with the most armored SUVs from World War II. We climbed in, and we could tell that even he had a hard time steering it!

We were all over Accra that day. We took in the seaside at Jamestown, visited the National Theatre, where we played the larger-than-me drums, and went to the National Museum, where we learned about Ghanaian history. We ended our day with dinner at Captain Hook's, which was an upscale seafood restaurant.

But, surprisingly, the owner was from Texas. He scurried around the restaurant in his cowboy boots, supervising staff and chatting with customers.

⊕

The next day at the hostel, I met a young lady who would become a close friend. Her name was Joy. She was very friendly — and she was an Ashesi student.

Taking a taxi to Ashesi everyday was not what I had imagined, so I worked up the courage to ask Joy if she knew of a short walking route to campus. She said she did. I liked her British accent and I wanted to make a friend, so I also asked her if I could walk with her the next day. She agreed. We settled on 7:00 am as our departure time. I felt a little selfish though, because I knew Kayt would never stand for leaving that early!

The next morning I awoke ready for the walk. I told Kayt about the arrangement I'd made with Joy, and Kayt said she'd just take a taxi. Joy and I met up a little after seven and started walking. We passed through the police barracks, where the police lived with their families, who were outside hustling and bustling. Children were brushing their teeth, and women were trying to sell candy.

The barracks were in poor condition, and, although I should have felt safe, I was actually pretty scared. It was very early in the morning, but I was nervous walking through their community — it was theirs. *What gave me, an American, the right to walk through their 'hood?* Surely anyone that looked at me knew I wasn't Ghanaian! Or so I thought. But no one said anything to Joy or me! They just looked at us and went about their day.

Soon my body was telling me we'd walked a long way because I was starting to sweat a lot. I knew I could stop the sweat if we slowed our walk, but I dared not say anything to Joy since, after all, I had asked if I could walk with *her*. After about twenty minutes of walking in the hot African sun, we arrived at Ashesi. I was surprised to learn that Joy would be working in the same building as I. She was a work-study student working as a receptionist. She really was nice and polite. Even though the sun was hot and I sweated, I decided I would walk with Joy each day for the rest of the week.

Dr. Hills told us that we would have a four-day week because there was a faculty and staff retreat scheduled for Friday. Of course, we were ecstatic! We immediately started planning our three day weekend. Then reality hit us. We had a lot of work to do, and we had to get through that Monday, Tuesday, Wednesday, and Thursday.

As we did research for our project, we learned that Ashesi had once used a student records management system (SRMS) named OSIS, but it had failed. We needed to investigate what went wrong and what Ashesi hoped for in a future SRMS system. We spent Monday scheduling a series of interviews. It was important for us to talk to users of OSIS, users of the current Excel-based system, and possible users of the new SRMS. Our interviewees included faculty, deans, staff, and even the Ashesi president. We asked a slew of questions, including the following:

- Did you use OSIS? In what capacity?

- What were the major difficulties you encountered with OSIS?

- How is student information currently managed at Ashesi? Which is paper based? Which is electronic?

- Tell us about Ashesi using Excel. When did that begin? What are the current categories you use in the existing student records spreadsheet? How do you share the data?

- Who has access to students' information entered into the spreadsheet? Are mechanisms in place to ensure data security?

- How do you currently share student information with others who need access? Can files be shared internally?

- Are you aware of any dependencies between the spreadsheet and any other business systems? What are they?

- In your opinion, what are the problems with using Excel?

- What do you want from the new system? What is its ideal functionality, in your view?

By the end of the week, we had interviewed about 15 people, and we began to understand why the previous system had failed. Carol was our most important interviewee. She commanded respect, and, although we weren't sure how our project would progress, we wanted her to approve all of our plans. Dr. Hills insisted that we immediately review the consulting plan with Carol. We set up a meeting with her, and Dr. Hills sat in. She gave us a green light to proceed, agreeing that we use this consulting model:

1. Establish a relationship

2. Explore organization broadly

3. Understand underlying problems/opportunities

4. Consider alternatives

5. Assess impact and sustainability and filter by feasibility

6. Create a scope of work and work plan

7. Implement work plan

8. Document outcomes

9. Make recommendations

10. Compile a final report

11. Final presentation

Our deliverables were to be:

1. Organizational assessment
2. High level alternatives analysis
3. Scope of work and work plan
4. Final report
5. Final presentation
6. Training materials

Wednesday was not a day that Kayt and I looked forward to. It was the day Dr. Hills would leave. Neither of us had really gotten to know any Carnegie Mellon faculty while we were in school, but it had been great getting to know Dr. Hills. He was always warm, and he looked forward to hanging out with us. Of course, we didn't mind because he would always treat us to dinner! And he offered such wonderful advice concerning our project. He had, after all, done this sort of thing many times before.

We had our farewell dinner at his hotel restaurant. We weren't really eager to eat, so we sat at the bar and just talked for over an hour. There were random tidbits of conversation. CNN news was on a flat screen TV nearby. One of the headlines was the rumored concession of U.S. presidential candidate Hillary Clinton. Of course, we talked about that.

At one point Kayt went to the restroom, and it gave me the opportunity to talk with Dr. Hills one-on-one. I was nervous sitting next to the INI's first director, but his relaxed demeanor put me at ease. He humbly revealed that he had been chief information officer of both CMU and the University of Alaska, and that he held appointments as Distinguished Service Professor at CMU and *Profesor Extradordinario* at the *Universidad Austral de Chile*. I was awed by his titles, but what was so striking to me was his selflessness. He had an honest desire to help Kayt and me.

A few days earlier I'd casually mentioned to him that I was the first black female graduate of the INI. (I would learn years later that this wasn't quite true and that at least one other black female had preceded me. But it was what I thought at the time.) Dr. Hills looked at me with a smile and said, "So you're the first black woman to graduate from the INI?" His tone indicated it was not really a question, but more of a statement that needed confirmation.

I responded with a smile, "Yes, I am."

He extended his hand for a handshake, and we shook. That one handshake was validation for me. It was a highlight of my trip.

Cape Coast is a city where African slaves were imprisoned before being shipped to the Americas. Kayt and I traveled there by bus, and it was a three-hour trip. It was our first time outside Accra, and we were excited.

At the bus station we were bombarded by a million taxi drivers looking for customers. Kayt and I hated moments like these! Luckily, two other foreigners agreed to share a taxi with us. Once the taxi reached the city limits, they were eager to sightsee, so they dropped us at our hotel.

Since it was about 11:00 am and we'd been up since 5:30 am, we anxiously placed orders at the hotel's seaside restaurant. We were a bit disappointed with the lunches themselves, but we were able to witness an amazing and exciting sight.

Right there on the Gulf of Guinea, we watched men boating in the distance. They engaged the water with respect, and they looked so small in the face of something so vast. They worked to haul a fishing net to shore, and it required the strength of about 30 of them! It was amazing to see their bare feet in sync as they sang a traditional work song. The sight reminded me of how

U.S. "colored" inmate gangs sang such songs as they laid railroad tracks and dug ditches in the 1930s and 1940s.

Our next stop was the slavery museum, but it didn't impress me much. A lot of it looked like a reproduction of the National Museum in Accra. But the slave dungeons...well, "impressed" isn't the right word. I was moved beyond measure.

Kayt and I visited a slave castle at Cape Coast.

As we entered a dungeon, a small light illuminated the walkway. *This light couldn't have been here 200 years ago!* Instantly, the tour guide shut it off. The only remaining light came from a small peep hole. *We are in the same dungeon where my ancestors were held, with no light, just like them.* The difference was that I was fully clothed, unshackled, and free to leave anytime.

One of the dungeon rooms was no larger than my bedroom, yet hundreds of men were sardined together in that room for several months at a time. (Women were kept in a separate dungeon.) We saw canal-like crevices in the floor that were built for the flow of urine and feces. I tried to imagine what it was like...how it smelled...how it sounded.

I reflected on how Europeans then believed that such barbarism was absolutely OK, and I began to get angry. I looked around at the others on the tour, and most were of European descent. *What emotions are they feeling? Surely theirs can't be like mine!*

Then I snapped back to reality. I looked at Kayt and thought of how 200 years ago she would have had dominion over me. Never could we have walked together, laughing and talking, seeing each other as equals. I realized that only courageous Europeans visited the castle. Courageous ones could face the barbarism that their ancestors had condoned and even advocated.

Members of the African diaspora, of which I am a part, were courageous too. Being in that place re-created my personal link to Africa, connecting me to my ancestors who had crossed the Atlantic.

We left the dungeon and went to a private cell, like "the hole" in U.S. prisons. This was the place where defiant captives were kept, only to die. They were chained in that small place. We saw scratches on the concrete walls that they had made with their bare hands! Then we headed to the "Door of No Return," which was the door through which captives had left the castle and boarded slave ships. Through that door was the ocean — the very same ocean that my ancestors had unwillingly sailed. It was a sobering moment.

Although dozens of similar "castles" dotted the Ghanaian coast, I wondered if *this* was the one from which my ancestors had left. If so, I was walking the same ground that they had walked hundreds of years earlier.

Slaves passed through this "Door of No Return" on the way to America.

⊕

Back in Accra, Kayt and I quickly got back into "work mode." We communicated with SRMS vendors in order to decide if any of them would be right for Ashesi. By the middle of week four, we had completed our second deliverable, "Analysis of Alternatives," and shared it with Carol. The document was a comprehensive survey of all of the SRMS options available to Ashesi, and we fit each SRMS into one of three categories: commercial, custom-built, and open source.

But we did not endorse any particular SRMS because we did not want to bias Ashesi. We planned to obtain demo copies of many SRMSs so that we could conduct user tests with the faculty, staff, and students. After the tests were complete, we would make a recommendation.

By the end of week four, we had completed our third deliverable, "Scope of Work," and we had shown that to Carol, too. (Yes, we were rockin' and rollin'!) This document showed that our formal SRMS recommendation would be backed by tons of research.

⊕

I had gained a bit of confidence by learning how to take the local bus system, but one day, I didn't feel up to the challenge and just decided to take a taxi. I told the driver "Danquah Circle."

Traveling by taxi was a game. Drivers would deliberately overcharge riders who they knew were foreigners, but locals could usually get a fair price. My strategy was to say as little as possible, so as not to give away my foreign-ness. I sat nervously in the car, wondering how much this guy would charge me.

As we approached Danquah Circle, he asked me for directions in the local Twi language. I couldn't act like I didn't understand him. If I did, he'd know I wasn't from Accra. So I just said the only thing I could say, "Where the fuel station is." He seemed to understand that and did a U-turn toward the fuel station. As we got closer, he said something else in Twi while pointing his finger at the fuel station. I just responded, "Yes, here sir." He calmly pulled over to let me out.

I knew that most locals, upon reaching a destination, would give the driver the amount of money they felt the ride was worth. This gave the rider the upper hand. But foreigners seemed to negotiate the fare before riding, which gave the driver the upper hand. I felt the ride was worth two cedi, so I handed the driver two one-cedi bills, hoping he wouldn't try to negotiate with me. And he took it! He didn't say anything! I was amazed. *Did I just pass for a local?!*

Kayt and I continued sightseeing, experiencing and enjoying as much of Ghana as we could. We attended "Street Dance

Africa" at the National Theatre, which was like the American show "So You Think You Can Dance?" but with a stronger hip-hop feel. I also spent more time with Joy.

Kayt and I went to a show at Ghana's National Theater.

Kayt and I eventually learned that Accra had a shopping mall, and we checked it out. It was awesome! The interior was modern, and we were free from the hassle of vendors trying to sell us stuff. Plus, the department store called "Game" had as much milk chocolate as I could stomach. I was in heaven!

Carol observed our eagerness to experience Ghana, so she invited us to a music festival. One of the acts was "Ken and Band," and they were awesome. They reminded me of Earth, Wind & Fire. We were also privileged to see some African dance, and, to my surprise, Joy sang in a gospel choir.

The day after the festival, we went to the Ghana Black Stars vs. Gabon Panthers soccer game, which was a World Cup qualifying match. I had never been to a soccer game, but I hollered and cheered for the Black Stars like any other fan! We sat with Nana, a friend from CMU, and had lots of fun.

On the fashion front, Kayt knew a lot about African fabrics and attire. I was impressed. One day we spotted a man wearing traditional garb, and Kayt said, "That's what most men in Cameroon wear every day. It's called a *bubu*."

Really? OK. Then I asked her what the women called theirs. "A *mumu*," she responded. I thought my ears had fooled me, so I asked her again. She responded a second time, "A *mumu*." *What?! She couldn't be serious!* I told her that some of my relatives used that word to refer to oversized house dresses.

Later I asked Joy about it. "Joy, the men call theirs a *bubu*, right?" "Yes, yes," she responded. "And the women call theirs a *mumu*?" She thought about it, as if retrieving a distant memory. Then suddenly she said, "Yes, yes, it's a *mumu*."

Now I was really in disbelief. I had been no more than five years old when I first heard the word "*mumu*." Scenes of being at MawMaw's house in the summertime replayed in my mind. Aunt Betty, MawMaw's sister, had not started working full-time yet. She would regularly come to MawMaw's, and they would shell peas together. They would laugh, joke, and gossip. They would sometimes be barefoot…but they would always be wearing what Aunt Betty called a "moomoo." Of course, at 5 years old, I thought "moomoo" was just a word they had made up. I could even remember MawMaw's elderly neighbor, Mrs. Piccola, using the word "moomoo." That was pretty much all she wore. She even made one for me when I was in the third grade.

All of those memories played in my head when Joy said, "Yes, yes, it's a *mumu*." At that moment, I realized I knew only a tiny fraction of African history, despite my study of slavery, reading books like *Amistad*, and watching movies like *Sankofa*. Studying, reading, and watching had taught me only so much. But Joy's

"Yes, yes, it's a *mumu*" was so empowering for me. It reinforced my connection to Africa.

🌐

By the end of week five, Kayt and I had completed another deliverable, "Interim Recommendations," and we showed it to Patrick. We realized that the system we would recommend could fail, as OSIS had, if Ashesi didn't address certain issues. We recommended that they make some immediate changes: 1) upgrade their local area network, 2) increase communication among faculty and staff concerning registration, 3) rehab their pre-registration process, and 4) enhance the student experience by improving communication concerning policies and processes.

We had been in contact with almost every SRMS vendor on our list, and some of the companies provided us with documentation, client testimonials, and sample contracts. The testimonials were important, so we reached out to those clients and got their feedback. For the companies that did not provide testimonials, we were able to find schools that were using their systems, and we contacted those clients as well. We received both positive and negative feedback.

In preparation for the demo tests we planned to run, we got some of the SRMSs running on our laptops. We tried them ourselves and recorded our own impressions. Then, from the end of week six to the end of week seven, we scheduled demo sessions with faculty, staff, and students. We asked the participants to complete specific tasks using the SRMS software, and we privately assigned scores based on how well each participant completed tasks on each system. We had separate score sheets for faculty, administrators, students, and IT personnel.

At the conclusion of our usage tests, we had a clear winner, so we immediately began to prepare the final presentation that would include our recommendation. We also enlisted the help of Kwame, a Swarthmore College student in Ghana for the summer, to assist us in writing a document we had promised to deliver. Kwame was eager to help us in any way he could.

Our final presentation was scheduled for week eight. It was our big moment, and we were ready. This was important to Ashesi. Carol, two deans, the IT staff, the assistant registrar, and many faculty members attended. We saw a clear front-runner, and they did, too. Carol immediately gave us the green light to proceed with the SRMS we recommended. We had hit a home run!

Also during the presentation, we reiterated the need for Ashesi to upgrade its local area network. Without an upgrade, intermittent network access for faculty, staff, and students could cause frustration and lead to the failure of the new SRMS. We also recommended that on-site support for the SRMS be contracted out to Gyamfi, one of the computer science faculty members. Gyamfi had developed his own SRMS, and he understood the details of a system like the one we recommended. We discussed with him his interest in supporting the system after our departure, and he was willing to ensure that it was implemented correctly and used effectively. We were relieved that he would support the new SRMS.

After our presentation Carol wasted no time, immediately making contact with the SRMS company and asking them to come to Ashesi to do on-site training. The company later agreed to do three days of training during the first week of September. All financial aspects of the project were within Carol's domain, and she handled them flawlessly.

The SIS users, Carol, Gyamfi, the Ashesi IT staff, Kayt, and I had truly worked as a team. Kayt and I were overjoyed that we had finished successfully (and two weeks early!) and that we had ensured the new SRMS would be sustainable. It was now time for us to step aside and let Ashesi take over.

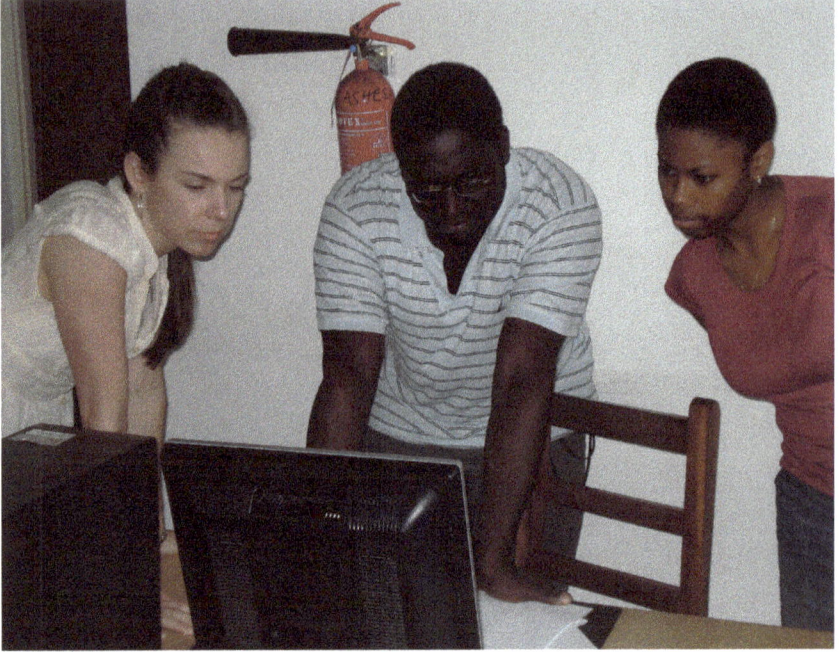

Kayt and I often worked with computer science instructor Gyamfi.

We continued to enjoy Accra, experiencing the sights and sounds of the city. We shopped for handicrafts at the Arts Centre, and a major part of the Arts Centre experience was talking to the shop owners. I met Faisal, who specialized in wood carvings. I also met Atuah, who was from the northern part of Ghana. He had received scars on his face as a baby, which marked him a part of the Frafra tribe. His trade was making leather handbags. Abu, who had been a boxer in his younger days, had a shop with a variety of goods. He was a Muslim with several wives. He asked me to marry him. I just laughed!

We were also invited to the home of Dr. Nana Apt, Ashesi Professor of Sociology and Dean of Academic Affairs. I wanted to be on my best behavior — Dr. Apt was an international scholar and she commanded respect. She lived on the northwest outskirts of Accra in an area known as McCarthy Hill, which really *was* suburbia. Almost every dwelling was a single-family home with a yard. One could even catch a glimpse of the beautiful Weija Reservoir in the distance.

When we arrived, Dr. Apt and her household staff eagerly welcomed us. Her cook began to prepare lunch for us, which gave us the opportunity to talk intimately. Dr. Apt trusted us, and she shared some personal stories. Then it was time to eat. The menu was awesome — yam, boiled plantain, fish, and *kontomire* (greens stew) with boiled eggs and okra. It tasted as great as it looked! But it was soon time to depart, and we memorialized the event with a photo.

Later the same day I went out with some new friends. Mayisha, a Spelman classmate, had been in Ghana the previous year as a Watson Fellow and had made some friends while there. She connected me with one of her friends, a guy who was named Nana. He came to the hostel that night and picked me up. He had two friends with him, Neil and Sammy. We all went to Labadi Beach, got a few drinks, and just relaxed. A street vendor was grilling goat kabobs. They tasted great!

After the beach Nana drove us around Accra. As we waited in traffic, we saw a troupe of acrobats doing a show in the street. Nana parked the car so we could watch the show. They were doing flips and other tricks. It really *was* a street party. There were lots of people, so we stopped to dance and have some fun.

The next day was Sunday, and I went to church with Joy. She was Catholic. I had attended a Catholic church only once before. Their rituals were odd to me because my roots were in the Baptist church. Nonetheless, I got spiritual nourishment at her church. I remember one line from the sermon saying that the Kingdom of Heaven was like "a treasure hidden in a field."

The next day, Monday, I went to a funeral. Madame Claudia, who catered the lunches at Ashesi, invited me to accompany her because she had observed my eagerness to experience the culture.

Among other stops on our final round of sightseeing,
we visited the Nkrumah Memorial, which honors Kwame Nkrumah,
Ghana's first president.

We agreed to meet at the home of the deceased person's family, the traditional place for a wake in Ghana. The deceased was a young woman named Rema. She had recently married but had died while giving birth. Madame Claudia knew the young lady and her parents, but she didn't know them well. Nonetheless, Madame Claudia wanted to pay her respects.

Ghanaian funerals go on for days. And they're huge! Entire neighborhoods attend, even people who don't know the deceased. This was the case at Rema's funeral, and droves of people surrounded the house. Each went in to say encouraging words to the parents and to give gifts. We did the same. Everyone in the crowd wore red and black, or just black. After the body was removed from the home and en route to the funeral site, we took a taxi there.

The funeral itself was not very different from those I had attended at home, but it was very long. We left early, and I thanked Madame Claudia for the experience.

⊕

My time in Ghana was almost over. I had already gotten souvenirs for my family and friends, but I wanted to get something extra special for my mom and sister. I decided to have Ghanaian clothes custom-made for them and asked them to send me their measurements.

I bought the fabric and explained to local seamstress Efua what I wanted for them. She had made a dress for me some weeks before, and I loved it! I asked her to make dresses for them that would be identical to mine. I also sketched a pantsuit and asked her to make that for them, too. I said I needed everything by the next week.

Wednesday, August 6 would be my last day in Accra. My flight was at 9:00 pm, and I spent the day doing last minute errands. I picked up the clothes from Efua, said goodbyes to my Ashesi colleagues, bought last minute gifts, and got my last haircut. I wanted to look great when I got home.

Back at the hostel, Kayt and I said our goodbyes. She would be traveling to Cameroon before returning to the U.S. She planned to do some non-profit work there and also catch up with her friends.

Ashesi's driver Peter soon arrived to take me to the airport. It was finally time to go. I reflected during the car ride. Part of me truly wanted to stay. I really liked Ghana, and I wasn't ready to leave. As Peter drove, I was tempted to tell him to take me back. I didn't have the guts though.

Then I was at the airport. I reluctantly checked in for my flight, went through customs, and waited to board. Before I knew it, I was in Amsterdam — and then back home.

I remember my first shower after returning home…the water was hot! I had been showering in cold water for months, and I was glad to have that warm-water feeling back. The hot water felt so good!

Aside from the hot water, my adjustments were few. I started working almost immediately, but I continued to think about Ghana. It had occupied a piece of my heart, and I knew I wanted to return. I promised myself I would move there someday.

Dr. Hills and I stayed in contact. He added me to his mailing list and began to send me photos of the international trips that his work required. He went to Chile each fall to teach at the *Universidad Austral de Chile*. I already thought the man was awesome, but then I learned that he could speak Spanish. I couldn't believe it. *What can't this man do?!*

In early 2009 Dr. Hills told me that he would be doing the orientation for the 2009 TCinGC volunteers, who would soon be leaving for their assignments. (Joe Mertz was away, teaching in Qatar.) To my surprise, Dr. Hills invited me to participate in one of the orientation sessions for the volunteers. He wanted me to describe the Ashesi project and my Ghana experience.

I looked forward to going back to CMU because I hadn't visited the university since I graduated. My roommate Donna agreed to travel with me, and Dr. Hills arranged hotel accommodations for us near the university. I was thankful and honored for the opportunity to do a presentation, but the paid expenses were a bonus.

Dr. Hills wanted my presentation to go well. He asked me to run through it with him, and we arranged to meet before the orientation. It was great seeing him! He liked my presentation. Later I met the new group of volunteers and gave my presentation. They were pumped, excited to do impactful work! Even Donna was inspired.

Back home in the Washington, DC area, Donna hipped me to a group that hosted and coordinated D.C. area social events. I joined the group's mailing list, and, to my surprise, they were soon sponsoring an event at the Ghanaian Embassy. *Ghanaian Embassy?!* I had to go!! I quickly purchased a ticket.

I was soooo excited to attend "An Evening at the Ghana Embassy." I knew exactly what I would wear — the Ghanaian dress I had had custom made. The Ghanaian Ambassador kicked off the event with a welcome and invited everyone to have some Ghanaian food. There was *jollof* rice, steamed fish, *banku*, and goat. I was in heaven! The delegation played local music and showed a film about places to visit in Ghana. There was even a drumming lesson. They succeeded in getting folks excited about the country I had already come to love.

That event really lit a fire under me. My interest in the country was renewed…and so was my memory of some of its ills. Like Oaxaca, Ghana had a water problem. But not only was Ghana's tap water not potable, its water infrastructure was unreliable. When one turned on the faucet, there was no guarantee that water would come out. *Why was the infrastructure so unreliable? Can technology help solve this problem?*

I soon learned about the Fourth International Conference on Appropriate Technology, which would be held in Ghana during Thanksgiving week 2010. *If I go, I can bounce ideas off the attendees and identify which ones are reasonable solutions!*

The conference website defined "appropriate technology" as that which "is designed with special consideration to the environmental, ethical, cultural, social, and economical aspects of the community it is intended for... [It] typically requires fewer resources, is easier to maintain, and has a lower overall cost and less of an impact on the environment compared to industrialized practices."

Also on the website was information about abstracts. The deadline was June 15. *Can I write an abstract? Will it be good enough?* This was a time to think big. I submitted an abstract and anxiously waited for July 1, which was to be the notification date. July 1 passed, and I didn't hear anything. I was disappointed.

I emailed the selection committee to inquire about the status of abstract reviews, and a few days later, they responded and told me that my abstract had been accepted. I couldn't believe it! *I wasn't crazy — my idea was reasonable!*

Now was the hard part — writing a complete research paper. The best ones would be selected for oral presentations, and the remainder would be selected for poster presentations. I nervously submitted my full paper on August 15 and then awaited the committee's decision.

The committee notified me on September 20 that I had been selected for a poster presentation. I had hoped to be selected for an oral presentation, but I was still very excited. I was going back to Ghana! I invited Mom, Grandmother, and my friend Sherwyn to join me.

With only two months before the conference, we were pressed to finalize our travel arrangements, with the first order of business being to purchase plane tickets. I chose KLM, of course! I later disseminated immunization information and insisted that my guests have their shots. Then, it was on to the passports and visas. And I registered everyone for the conference.

The biggest hurdle was finding an appropriate hotel because the time zone difference complicated my telephone calls to hotels in Accra. Many of the hotels had only two twin beds in each room, and that wasn't adequate for our group. Eventually, I found a reasonably priced hotel that had a two queen bed setup. We were finally set.

We arrived in Ghana the weekend prior to Thanksgiving. I was back!

I was nervous though. What Mom, Grandmother, and Sherwyn knew of Africa was only what I had told them and, unfortunately, what they had learned from TV. I very much hoped that their experience would be a positive one. I hadn't brought them to Africa to have a bad experience.

We had just settled into the hotel when Mom wanted to shower, and she told me there was no hot water. We had been assured by the hotel that there was hot water, and there was a hot water tank in the bathroom to prove it. I reasoned it might take a while for the water to get hot, so I told Mom that I would shower first, giving the water ample time to warm up for her.

But, as I showered, I noticed that the water didn't get any warmer. I had no choice but to shower with cold water during my time there in 2008, but I didn't want that for them! I dreaded stepping out of the bathroom and telling Mom and the others that the hot water didn't work. It would start the trip on a bad note. But I had no other choice. I had to tell them.

My mom was upset — she couldn't believe we didn't have hot water. I was embarrassed. As Mom took her shower, I had to figure out something. I went to the front desk and they told me I would have to turn the hot water tank on.

Turn it on, ehh? I ran back to the room to try to spare Mom any further torture. I found a switch on the tank and pushed it. We ran the water for a little while, and, sure enough, it began to get hot. I was sooo relieved! Without ever having used a tank before, I had no way to know how to operate it. I would never have figured it out in a million years.

After the water incident, the trip got better. I brushed up my taxi skills and got us a ride to the University of Ghana, where the conference was being held. We inspected the venue where posters were to be presented and then left for some sightseeing.

First, we went to Ashesi. I was anxious to show them my old "stomping grounds." I showed Mom, Grandmother, and Sherwyn the classroom buildings, the building where I had worked, and the cantina where I had eaten lunch every day.

Outside Carol's building I saw a young woman sitting outside on a bench. As I got closer to her, I could see that she looked a little like Joy, but with more hair. I had emailed Joy before I left the U.S. to let her know I'd be in town, but I never received an answer. *That girl can't possibly be Joy. She's the last person I expect to see.*

Then I realized that it *was* Joy. I stopped dead in my tracks and yelled, "JOYYYYYYYYYY"! She looked up from her laptop and looked at me. "Adrienne!" she yelled. She was in disbelief. She stood up and all I could do was yell her name, "Joy," again and again. I was filled with "joy" to see her. Then I hugged her…it was a long hug. We cried.

As much as I wanted to talk to my friend — a friend with whom I hadn't talked much in two years — I knew that she had school work to do. She knew that I understood, but I sensed she regretted not being able to seize the moment. So she reached into her book bag, pulled out a photo of herself, and gave it to me. I hugged her again and asked that she do better about keeping in touch. Then it was over.

I walked away, still in disbelief. I had managed to bump into the one person I thought I'd probably never see again. I know that God orchestrated the whole event. He is awesome!

Then it was off to see Patrick, the president of Ashesi. Dr. Hills had been working with Ashesi to plan the local area network and Wi-Fi system for Ashesi's new campus, but communication had dwindled. Dr. Hills hoped that I could remind Patrick about his willingness to help.

We sat in the library waiting area for an opportunity to speak with Patrick. He was always busy, so I was surprised that he was even on campus. The receptionist told him that visitors were waiting to see him. And we waited.

Finally, Patrick welcomed us to his office. I was a bit embarrassed to barge in with no prior appointment, but I was glad to see him. I think he, too, was surprised by my small delegation. I introduced him to my family, told him about the conference, invited him to attend, and passed on the message from Dr. Hills. Patrick was easygoing. I really liked him.

⊕

The conference opened with an evening reception at a small technical school downtown. Tables and chairs were set out in the courtyard, and there was a buffet of Ghanaian cuisine. An African dance troupe performed for us, and it was quite a sight! I was glad that Mom, Grandmother, and Sherwyn were able to see that.

Mom enjoyed the conference's opening reception.

Afterward, the DJ cranked up the music and everyone started dancing. Even Grandmother, who had been having hip trouble, was on the dance floor and had a good time. In fact, everyone had a good time.

The next day we went to the University of Ghana for the conference. I presented my poster and listened to several of

Grandmother had a good time on the dance floor.

the oral presentations. A special treat for me was the Ghana Minister of Water, who came to deliver a keynote address. I listened very intently to his points. I hoped I'd get a chance to talk to him one-on-one.

At lunch I spotted the Minister of Water alone. *Go for it, Adrienne!* I approached him and thanked him for his remarks. I wanted to know if the government welcomed ideas from the public on how to improve things, so I began telling him that I had ideas on how to make the water system more reliable. "If you have a good idea, let's talk about it," he said. His words were so encouraging, and they gave me confidence that the government would listen to any reasonable idea that was proposed. I had accomplished something that I never imagined possible — getting a green light from the Ghanaian government itself!

After the conference ended, I took my guests to the slave castle at Cape Coast. They were surprised by the number of street vendors that we saw en route, and they were also amazed at the size of the Accra metropolitan area. We visited a museum at the slave castle and then took a guided tour to the same castle that I had visited with Kayt two years earlier. It was a humbling and solemn experience for Mom, Grandmother, and Sherwyn. And, even though I had been there before, I shared those emotions with them, as if I were visiting for the first time.

The last destinations on our "must visit" list were the Kwame Nkrumah Memorial and the ultimate souvenir market, the Arts Centre. I reconnected with several of my friends and even convinced Atuah to have lunch with us.

Before we knew it, our week in Ghana had ended, and it was time to go home. Everything had turned out well, and I was so glad that my guests' experience was a good one.

⊕

To stay abreast of Ashesi happenings, I signed up for their e-newsletter. They had finally moved to their new campus, which was about 20 minutes north of Accra in Bekeruso. On the Ashesi website, I "virtually" toured the new campus. It was beautiful! And it was huge! There was a nice library, a building for faculty and staff offices, a computer lab building, a student center, dormitories, a sports complex, and a dining facility. And everything was brand new! I was so happy for them!

Also on Ashesi's website, I saw a link to login to the SRMS that Kayt and I had recommended. *Are my eyes fooling me? This is fall 2011.* We had made our recommendation in summer 2008 and Ashesi was now at a new campus with many more students. *Is Ashesi was still using the very same system? More than three years later?!* Well praise God! Kayt and I had done something right. To see that was very rewarding.

⊕

The year now is 2013, and I often reflect on my 2008 experience in Ghana. "Do you believe you really made a difference at Ashesi," a radio interviewer recently asked me. I responded, "Yes, I do…but I believe it made more of an impact in *my* life. It gave *me* confidence and helped me believe in *myself.* It helped me believe that I could do something big. It helped me believe that I could change the world."

Changing the world may sound cliché, but God gives each of us a purpose. Mine is to help make life better for others, and that's what I will keep trying to do.

CHAPTER SIX

PALAU 2009

YIXIN LIU

Scottish bagpipes played. Dressed in my graduation gown, I saw the seats of the stadium packed with parents, relatives and friends of the graduates. The members of the Kiltie band, Carnegie Mellon's marching pipe band, were dressed in full Scottish regalia, including kilts and knee socks. They led the graduating class to seats in the outdoor stadium. Carnegie Mellon is one of the few universities in the United States that offers a degree in bagpiping.

As I walked toward my seat, I thought about the journey that had taken me to that stadium. There were flashbacks of long nights studying, completing homework assignments, and working with teammates on projects and presentations. And memories of panic about university applications and financing my studies.

It seemed a long journey from my childhood to this graduation ceremony.

With an older brother and an older sister, I was the youngest child in our lower middle class family. My parents saved every penny possible. My mother was a housekeeper and my father a fish butcher. Neither of them had completed elementary school, and my siblings did not attend college. I made a resolution when I started my high school education. I wanted to be the first in my family to get a college degree — to make my family proud and, more importantly, to show that one can pursue a college degree in spite of one's financial circumstances.

My mum cooked three meals a day, seven days a week, to cut costs. Eating out or even ordering takeout was a luxury. One time, at the age of five, I missed the school bus to my pre-school. The school was a 15-minute ride from our house. So my mum and I walked for an hour to my school instead of taking public transportation. The sun was scorching in the hot and humid climate of Singapore. I carried my backpack of school materials, and my mum had my lunch box in one hand and an umbrella in the other hand to shield us from the sun.

My legs were tired and sore. And all this was to save less than two dollars in public transportation fare. Then my mum walked back home, covering twice the distance that I had. She showed me the importance of frugality.

Growing up, I wanted to become a doctor and help my family break out of our situation. I dreamed of holding a scalpel and being a surgeon, not just a physician. I wanted to help save lives and alleviate the suffering of patients. I wanted to help the sick and destitute. Perhaps coming from my background had enabled me to empathize more with the suffering of others. And watching American television shows like ER strengthened my resolve to be a doctor. I wanted to reduce the pain in the world.

But reality hit me when I took a biology course in middle school. The naming system used for the human anatomy was a nightmare for me. I had problems remembering the names, making references to them, and explaining how the human body's subsystems worked together. Animal dissection was my most dreaded part of school days because I had to endure the sight of blood and gore while learning about animals' body parts.

So I decided not to pursue medicine as a career. I searched within myself, asking what it was that I wanted in life.

After a period of soul searching, I found the answer. I still wanted to have an impact on lives, bringing a smile to a stranger's face and improving the well-being of others. I moved on to another area — technology.

The Internet boom and rapid expansion of information technology were in progress. I chanced upon ThinkQuest, an initiative by Oracle to encourage the use of Internet as a collaboration tool, to create educational websites and curricula for educators around the world, and to use them for teaching. ThinkQuest provided a platform for me to communicate with people from around the world. I felt empowered by the ability to share knowledge with people in other countries and participate in lively discussions and debates on issues ranging from environmental issues to world history.

It was a turning point and the catalyst that later led me to computer science and engineering. I started to read about and experiment with web development and content creation. Soon I was involved with technology-related school projects — creating websites, directing and editing videos, etc. I was known as the "geek" in my school.

I realized that technology is an empowering tool to share knowledge, create content, and share worthy causes like non-governmental organizations (NGOs) that help people in third world countries. Most importantly, I realized that, through technology, I could help make a difference in the lives of others. I even created educational websites about organ transplants and human anatomy, using animation to help explain human bodily processes and functions, and I did this in spite of my earlier decision to abandon medical studies.

I had never flown in an airplane. In fact, my family had never traveled out of Singapore, our tiny island nation with a land area of only 274 square miles. Traveling was an indulgence beyond our reach.

But I wanted to travel overseas. I wanted to see the world out there and experience the four seasons. (Singapore is a tropical country with summer weather all year.) I wanted to see other natural landscapes and how other people live and interact. To quote American anthropologist Margaret Mead, "As the traveler who has once been from home is wiser than he who has never left his own doorstep, so a knowledge of one other culture should sharpen our ability to scrutinize more steadily, to appreciate more lovingly, our own." I envied my classmates, who shared travel stories of interesting places, cities, mountains, lakes, and beaches they visited.

When I entered high school, my goal was to pursue a university education abroad. What better way to get a taste of life overseas? In my last year of high school I took various college admissions tests, including the SAT, wrote personal essays, and applied to schools overseas. Though I was accepted to several universities, my financial background haunted me. How would I be able to finance my living expenses, school tuition fees and other expenses? I applied to various funds, organizations and programs. At last I managed to secure a full sponsorship from the Singapore government for my overseas education. I was over the moon.

I arrived at Carnegie Mellon University to pursue my undergraduate degree in electrical and computer engineering. It was a dream come true: to study alongside the brightest minds from around the world at a place where the first wireless network was created, where a faculty member was credited with inventing the emoticon, and where science and technology were at the forefront of the university's research. I had the best of both worlds, access to arts and music programs and performances at the College of Fine Arts, and also access to state-of-the-art computer laboratories at the School of Computer Science.

Carnegie Mellon students are motivated, driven, and goal-oriented. Everyone knows that everyone else has worked hard to get there. But the community is supportive and nurturing. I was soon involved in student organizations like Habitat for Humanity, Alternative Spring Break, and Development Solutions Organization, all of which were making a difference to the lives of others and having an impact on the community.

When I was a third-year student, I wanted to do something different, something that allowed me to have a direct impact on a community. I saw a flyer on a bulletin board that described the Technology Consulting in the Global Community (TCinGC) program. I soon talked to the program director, Professor Joe Mertz, and, after hearing what he had to say, I was sold on the program. It seemed a perfect match for me. I applied and was accepted.

In TCinGC I would be able to make a direct contribution to a partnering organization. I would be able to have face-to-face interaction with the people I would help by advising them on a technological solution to help them fulfill their mission. I would be able to get my hands dirty, actually implement my recommendation, and then see the impact first-hand.

But my friends had questions. Why would you want to spend a summer in a remote place? Why not get yourself an internship with a company or an institution? Don't you need to get a job after graduation? These were some of their questions. But I decided to follow my heart. The opportunity to travel to a developing country and utilize technology to help them out was appealing. And it was a chance to rekindle the passion I had when I was younger — to help others.

Professor Mertz asked if I would accept an assignment to the Republic of Palau to help the Ministry of Education with IT infrastructure and management. But I wondered "Where is Palau? Would I really be able to do this alone? Would I even be able to survive for all of the ten-week assignment? Were there other projects or assignments available?"

I did some research and soon found that the assignment would be a good fit for me. I had worked as a high school math substitute teacher before starting my undergraduate education, an experience that would help me understand the needs and challenges faced by the Palau Ministry of Education. I accepted Joe's offer to work on the project.

An orientation class was held about two months before the project started. In the class there were other students headed to projects in other places. We learned about the TCinGC consulting model, which was based on a "helping relationship," where the consultant works with the client and continuously involves the client in the process. This is different than working for the client strictly as an expert. We wouldn't "parachute in" to recommend solutions. Instead we would involve our client in the consulting process so that there would be buy-in for the recommended solution. This would help to ensure that the solution would be accepted and used by the client, even after we left the country. The orientation sessions also taught us about health, visas, security and safety in the developing world.

⊕

My project was to start one week after the beginning of the summer break. I went home to Singapore to visit my parents before the project start. I was really excited and glad to see their faces again — I had been away for two years. But my plan to spend the summer in Palau soon met strong resistance. With the outbreak of the 2009 swine flu pandemic, new cases had been in the headlines of Singapore's daily newspaper and television news channel. My parents were concerned, especially about the safety and hygiene conditions in Palau and the risk of travelling there. They voiced their concerns again and again.

But I had just finished reading Carnegie Mellon Professor Randy Pausch's *The Last Lecture*, and I knew that I had to press on. Professor Pausch's lecture and book talked about running into a "brick wall." I felt that I had stumbled into just such a brick wall. But this was not going to stop me from completing the program. I was not going to give up this opportunity to do development work.

Family dinners became negotiation sessions as I debated with my parents about the trip. After much time spent reassuring them that I would be able to take care of myself, I finally caught my flight to Palau.

⊕

I could smell the moisture in the air as I arrived at Palau International Airport. Most people at the airport arrival hall were wearing face masks because of the swine flu pandemic. But I wasn't concerned. There had so far been no known cases of swine flu in Palau.

At the Palau airport I met up with Tom Lewkowitz, a Carnegie Mellon computer science major and my partner for the project at the Palau Ministry of Education. Edwel, the systems administrator at the Ministry, was there to receive us. "*Alii* (a-LEE). (Hello.) Welcome to Palau!" he said.

I'll never forget the smile on his face. Edwel was vivacious and happy. He shook our hands. He was a stout guy with a short mustache and beard. Well versed in programming, web development and computer networks, Edwel would be our main point of contact for the project. He showed us to his car and helped us load our abundant luggage into its trunk.

We hopped in and drove to a local restaurant for breakfast. As we drove, I soaked up the sights and sounds of Palau: stray dogs roaming freely along the roads, chickens walking and pecking, and fruit trees, including trees of mango, banana, papaya and *rambutan* (a red, hairy tropical fruit). Most houses were made of cement or wood topped with a tin roof. The blue sky reflected in the clear waters of Palau.

At the restaurant, I ate a big breakfast of *bangsilog*, which is fried vinegar-marinated milkfish, a fried egg, fried garlic rice and some side salads. This is a popular Filipino breakfast. Edwel said that Palauan food was strongly influenced by the food cultures of Japan, Taiwan and the Philippines. We used our time together to learn more about each other. We discussed topics ranging from family to tourism to the economy. We described traditions and festivities in our respective cultures. It was a bonding time, and we started to build a rapport and a sense of understanding of each other.

Tom and I soon found that the Internet speed available in Palau was far slower than the Internet we knew in the United States. I felt like I was back to using a dial-up connection. In Palau the Internet crawled. But we soon became accustomed to the slow service, and we were thankful for the ability to remain connected to our families and friends.

Tom Lewkowitz was my partner working
for the Palau Ministry of Education.

⊕

Settling into Palau wasn't a smooth process. There was a problem with our housing situation. Tom and I were put into a temporary accommodation at a motel in Palau. And, a week after our arrival in Palau, our accommodation was still not arranged. Were we going to stay in motels for the whole ten weeks? We had a problem.

But Dr. Alex Hills, senior advisor to the TCinGC program, flew into Palau at the end of our first week to make sure that we were doing OK. It was a great relief to see Dr. Hills. We knew that we would no longer be alone in working on our housing problem.

But first Dr. Hills arranged for Tom and me to meet with the other student team in Palau — Mi Gyeong Koo from Korea,

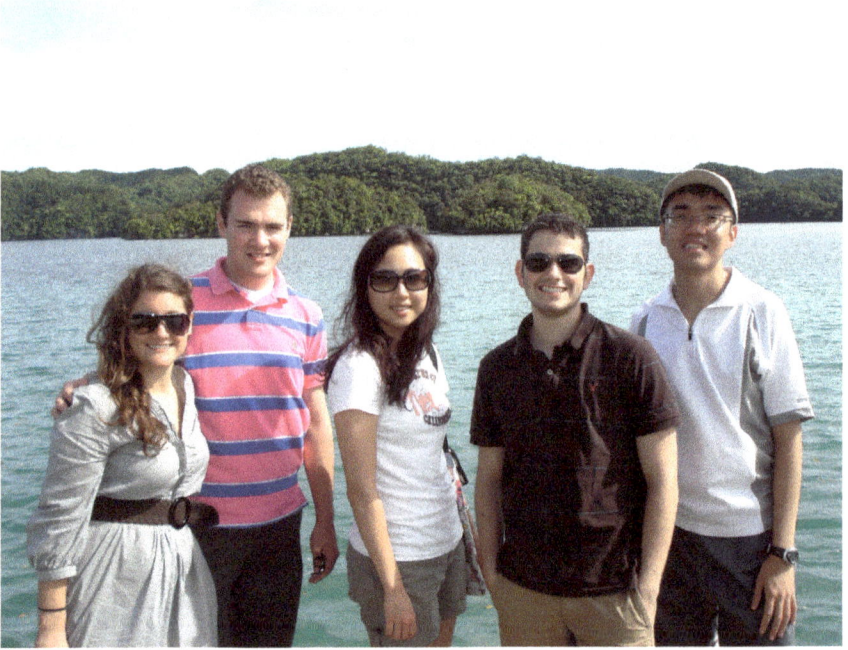

In all, there were five Carnegie Mellon student volunteers working in Palau that summer. From left to right, they were: Kate, Brandon, Mi, Tom and me.

Kate Edgar from Missouri, and Brandon Loughery from Virginia, who were all working at the Palau Ministry of Health. We found that they already had accommodation, an apartment that was close to our Ministry of Education office. We went to see their apartment. It was furnished with a sofa, a dining table, dining chairs and beds. It was ideal for volunteers there for only ten weeks.

Dr Hills had a meeting with managers of the Ministry of Education to discuss our housing issues. To our surprise, Dr Hills arranged for Tom and me to have an apartment in the same building as the other student team — just one floor below them! There happened to be a vacant apartment in the same building. It was perfect!

And that apartment was a dream home for me. I had my own kitchen equipped with a refrigerator, gas stove, microwave, oven, and, most importantly, air-conditioning for the whole apartment. This was a big deal in Palau, which is hot and humid all year round. The apartment really eased our transition to island living.

Dr Hills was the hero who helped Tom and me solve our housing problem. I still refer to him as "Captain America."

Dr Hills's visit also helped with the direction of our project. During a meeting with him and the management team at the Ministry of Education, we discussed project details like timeline, objectives and desired outcomes. This helped to establish a common understanding between us and leadership at the Ministry of Education. It proved to be critical during our remaining nine weeks in Palau.

⊕

During our first week in Palau, we spent time understanding the needs of the Ministry of Education. We shadowed a few of the administrators in the office, observing how they worked and understanding their workflow process. I studied the organizational structure of the Ministry and researched the elementary and middle schools that the Ministry supervises. At first my presence made some of the staff uncomfortable. In order to get them to share their internal workflow processes, I tried to break the ice, introducing myself and spending time talking and hanging out with them inside and outside the office. It was through these informal conversations that I gleaned the most information: what frustrated the staff, the tasks that occupied most of their time, the tasks that were particularly labor intensive, and how the staff members shared information among themselves and within the organization. These conversations were a great way to get more information about the staff and the way they operated.

And we worked with Edwel. In addition to being the systems administrator in the Ministry's central office, Edwel handled logistics and other jobs. When required, he was an operations

Tom and I worked in Palau's Ministry of Education building.

manager. He took on this additional work due to a shortage of manpower. But Edwel planned to retire after working five more years, and I knew that a proper succession plan was essential to ensure that his knowledge of the organization's technical infrastructure wouldn't be lost. Training would also be essential so that Edwel's replacement would be competent and comfortable handling IT administration for the Ministry.

During lunch times Tom and I talked things over. There were so many things we could do to help the Ministry to streamline the way they operated. We discussed student registration, course registration, student tracking, grade reporting and transcript generation. However, our main priority was the grade reporting system because it was the reason our assistance was originally requested. Still, we tried not to lose sight of the big picture. We tried to integrate as much information as possible to address the needs of the various departments within the Ministry.

I was surprised when I saw how data entry of the test responses of students was done. It was a labor-intensive process, with office administrators keying into Microsoft Excel the responses made by students in the nationwide standardized tests. Different administrators worked on different Excel files, and there was, at times, confusion when an Excel file had been updated by different administrators.

The responses of the students had already been shaded in on the answer sheets. And I found that the Ministry already had a scanner facility with preloaded software that would allow the responses to be captured. The scanner was not being used because its output file was not compatible with Microsoft Excel.

And this caused a huge bottleneck in this process. All that was needed was an application and interface that would allow administrators to use the scanner to capture the responses of the students and feed them into Microsoft Excel.

After our first week of consultation with Edwel, using a whiteboard to generate ideas, brainstorm and discuss, we decided to create a web-based information system to manage, analyze, and report student standardized test scores. Administrators were really excited about not having to do manual data entry. With this buy-in, Tom and I went ahead to develop a prototype of the system that we had proposed.

We set about coding our proposed system. Each week we shared our progress with Edwel and asked him for feedback. Tom and I had an increasing sense of satisfaction as we saw our system take form.

Every day we joined our colleagues for lunch in the office. We cooked using a rice cooker and usually had rice, noodles, eggs and canned food. Our daily lunch affair was something like a potluck, and I would sometimes contribute a few cans of sardines toward the meal. The meals were usually simple, but lunchtime was the perfect opportunity to interact with the staff on an informal basis.

We often shared a potluck lunch with the staff.

At the lunches I had the opportunity to learn more Palauan. I asked my colleagues to teach me common phrases, names and greetings. It allowed me to better fit into their community by speaking their language. And it put me in a better position when bargaining with the merchants in the market. As I learned about Palauan, it helped me to better appreciate my native language, which is Mandarin. As Johann Wolfgang von Goethe once said, "Those who know nothing of foreign languages know nothing of their own."

By the eighth week, it was time to roll out our work product and share with the staff the application we had developed. We organized a couple of training sessions to guide the administrators on the use of the application, which enabled them to create test result reports and track performance in specific areas as needed. For example, if the data showed that most students in a class had not scored well on questions related to English grammar, the teacher would be able to receive immediate feedback and spend more time on grammar during English classes. At the same time, administrators no longer had to key in student test responses. With the new application, the whole process, including grading, was automated.

Yet in spite of our training sessions and the user manuals we had created, we found that the application was still not well understood by the staff. There was apprehension and uncertainty about using it. But we still had about a week left. Tom and I spent the week working with the staff and administrators, sitting side by side with them and showing them how to use the application we had developed. An "aha!" moment, when each user finally understood and liked the new application, was a rewarding time for us.

I realized how important it had been to involve client partners early in the consulting and development process. A system can be built, but it has to be accepted by the users. They have to be comfortable with it. Although some procedures may have seemed intuitive to us, explaining the reasoning behind certain steps and functions — no matter how trivial — was critical to the success of the project.

I was happy with the improvements that we had made. The web-based information system was a huge improvement. I hadn't expected that we would have such a big impact. And the TCinGC experience has given me confidence that I can make a difference to others.

⊕

My ten weeks in Palau were spent not just on project work but also on exploring the island, making new friends, and reflecting about life.

I thought the best way to experience Palauan culture was to try the food and eat like the locals do. I ate some interesting and exceptional food, including fruit bat soup and turtle soup. The fruit bats were served whole (including the head, wings and feet) in a pot as a soup, where one could still see and feel the hairs on the wings of the bats as they were being consumed. But I also had one of the best delicacies that I could ask for — sashimi, which is especially fresh in Palau. I ate the raw fish with soya sauce and a light tinge of lime juice soon after the fish were caught. With each bite of sashimi, there came an explosion of flavor. The sashimi was so fresh that it melted in my mouth. Each bite released the flavor of the sea, complemented by the saltiness of the soya sauce and the sweet tang of the lime juice.

One of my most memorable experiences was a trip to Jellyfish Lake. Arriving at Eil Malk Island, I climbed over steep terrain and hiked into the woods, up a large limestone staircase and then down the other side to Jellyfish Lake. At first the lake looked like just any other. But, after I put on my snorkeling gear and peeked beneath the water, I saw millions of jellyfish. Some were as big as my hand, and some were as small as a thumb.

As I swam out into the lake, I had to push them away. They didn't sting, and it was OK to touch them. They had no tentacles, only cones. They had evolved without the ability to sting.

Palau is touted as one of the best diving sites in the world. All five of us Carnegie Mellon students signed up for a diving course.

Underwater I saw a myriad of wildlife — fishes of many colors — clownfish, zebrafish, puffer fish and others I was unable to name. The corals also came in a variety of colors — violet, green, blue, purple, orange, pink, yellow, white, brown, and black. I saw an oyster with a pearl in it. There were giant clams and sea cucumbers lying on the sea bed. When I opened my hand, a school of little blue fish came and tried to bite my fingers and palm.

We also managed to get close to some sharks, including a bull shark, gray reef shark, whitetip reef shark, oceanic whitetip, and silvertip shark. We also saw wahoo, tuna, hawksbill turtles, green turtles, eagle rays, giant groupers and barracuda.

In Palau the pace of life is much slower than in Singapore or in the big cities of the United States. There is no hustle and bustle — only the sound of wind chimes and leaves rustling. I grew to appreciate the changes in the sky during sunrise and sunset, during times of high tide and low tide, and during times of sunny weather and sudden thunderstorms followed by rainbows. I watched all this through the month, as the moon went from a full sphere to a thin crescent in the nighttime sky. And, with no interference from city lights, I could see the Milky Way galaxy.

Scenes like this are typical of Palau.

I felt close to nature. I was happy to sit by a lake and enjoy the breeze. Life was simple and happy without television and with only limited Internet and text message service. I woke up daily to the crowing of the roosters at the break of dawn. The melodies of birds chirping accompanied me daily as I walked to my office.

Betel nut chewing is common in Palau. People are often seen chewing betel nuts and carrying a container for spitting. A Betel nut is an acorn shaped nut. For chewing it's wrapped in a leaf and seasoned with lime, pepper, nutmeg, and some other spices. The chewer places the wrap in his mouth and chews it, spitting frequently. It's something like chewing tobacco.

In my last week in Palau, I decided to "do as the Palauans do" and give betel nut chewing a shot. I got a buzz as expected, but the experience was not the most pleasant because I had to frequently spit out the red-colored juice. But I gave it a try. I guess it took me a step closer to being a Palauan.

I felt emotions rising in my last few days in Palau. On one hand, I was looking forward to returning back to school, starting the new semester, and being back on familiar ground. But I found it hard to part with my new friends in Palau. We had shared a lot in our times together, our family life, our aspirations, and even our life values. But, as the saying goes, all good things must come to an end.

My last few days were spent hanging out with the friends I had made and the colleagues I had worked with at the Ministry of Education, exchanging contacts, writing farewell notes, and shopping for farewell gifts.

My ten weeks in Palau had a deep impact on my life: shaping new values, rethinking priorities, learning to deal with uncertainties and building my confidence to pursue international development work. Later my friends noticed a change in me. I was more mature, calmer, and more adventurous.

Back at Carnegie Mellon, I chuckled when the same friends who had advised me to consider a corporate internship for the summer complained about how "normal" their summers had been. I had many more stories to tell than they did.

I had learned to communicate much more effectively and, most importantly, to listen to others before expressing my own views. In Palau I listened to the concerns of my colleagues at the Ministry of Education, and I listened to how they communicated with each other and shared information. As a consultant, I put the clients in first position, listening to what they needed rather than building what I thought they needed.

In the past I had been task- and results-oriented. But during the summer I had become more process- and people-oriented. I was more mindful of the impact of my actions on other people, and it was evident in the project work I did during the school semester. When I led a project, instead of just asking my team-mates for the work they had done, I asked about the process they followed in doing the work, and I provided support if needed.

I also learned a different way to react when a problem arises. Instead of diving straight in to tackle the challenge, I learned to take a step back, look at the big picture, and see if there are alternative ways to approach the problem. Of course, this takes time. I used to joke about being on "Palauan time," but I found that it has helped me to be more productive and in control of situations than immediately reacting to events.

I traveled with a group of friends to Peru during the winter break after my return from Palau, and I found my TCinGC experience to be practical and useful. There was a series of unexpected events that occurred during our trip. There were times when our flights were delayed and times when some of my traveling buddies had altitude sickness or food poisoning. Most of them freaked out.

But I was able to maintain my cool and work on adapting plans to each surprise. I talked to and sought the help of Peruvian locals, who shared home remedies for my friends' altitude sickness and food poisoning. It didn't bother me that we didn't know where we were going to stay the next day. My experience in Palau had prepared me to expect the unexpected.

The TCinGC experience has become a part of my resume, and it has expanded my employment opportunities. This was especially true at job fairs and job interviews, where my multilingual and multi-cultural experience in TCinGC made me stand out. I have found that some employers place more emphasis on "soft skills" than technical knowledge.

I graduated from Carnegie Mellon, and I now work at a water utility in Singapore. In recent years, the United Nations has recognized that access to safe water and sanitation is a human right. At the water utility, I help to provide safe, clean, accessible and affordable drinking water and sanitation for Singapore's citizens. My long term goal is to do development work with an international organization.

After graduation, I was interviewed on the radio about my experiences in Palau.

And I have continued to remain active in community work. Recently I led a group visit to an orphanage in Batam, Indonesia, where most of the children lost their parents in the big earthquake in 2005. We spent time interacting with the children and understanding their needs, as well as assessing their living conditions. We hope to help increase awareness of their plight and encourage sponsors to each fund a child, providing proper accommodation, care and education at the orphanage. At the same time, I also volunteer with non-profit organizations on weekends, and, in my free time, I sometimes work on policy papers, proposals and projects.

The volunteering experience has made me realize that, while I may not be able to completely change the world with my actions, I am able to do small things that make a difference.

I hope to change the world — one step at a time.

CHAPTER SEVEN

TECHNOLOGY CONSULTING IN THE GLOBAL COMMUNITY

JOSEPH MERTZ

I find satisfaction in helping, and I think others do, too. People like to be in a position to help. The helping experience allows one to say "I guess I do know some stuff, and I guess I do have some value." Our students are valued as members of the Technology Consulting in the Global Community (TCinGC) program and as ambassadors of Carnegie Mellon University. But they are especially valued by people in the organizations where they work, the people they help day-to-day.

TCinGC is a ten-week summer program that places students as consultants to work in developing nations and under-resourced communities. They work with nonprofits, government ministries, non-governmental organizations, schools, and sometimes small businesses. Working with TCinGC is similar to doing an internship because it's a short-term work assignment. But it's different than a typical internship in some important ways. That's why we call participants "student consultants" and not "interns".

First, a student consultant is in a leadership position. In a typical internship, a student is assigned a project and closely supervised. But TCinGC student consultants work with organizations that are looking for help in understanding their technology problems and solving them. The student consultant leads the process of investigating the problem, articulating it, and recommending a solution. He or she then works with the client to implement the solution in a way that is sustainable.

As one TCinGC student consultant put it, "This was the REAL THING. I was plopped down on an island 20 miles around, 6,000 miles from home, with one other kid I'd never met before, and I was told to help fix their communication infrastructure."

A second way that student consultants are different is that they are provided substantial orientation and preparation, and they receive faculty advice as they work on the projects. They undergo an orientation process that helps them look deeply at what their work role will be and how they can be most effective in helping their clients arrive at valuable and sustainable outcomes. The orientation also addresses preparing to work in a different culture, travel logistics, language, professional behavior, workplace norms, and safety.

And third, student consultants use a well-defined consulting process, including specific deliverables — interim reports, status updates, and a final report. The consulting process helps to guide their work and communication with members of client organizations.

Student consultants have a much richer experience than those doing typical internships. They work on problems that affect real people and organizations, and their work is expected to have purpose and lasting value. It's not just a learning exercise.

A returning student consultant wrote: "Thanks to TCinGC, I was able to face my own weaknesses, challenge a real life problem, and propose a meaningful solution in an extreme environment. I have learned how to challenge the unknown and unexpected in an IT project. I also realized recently how hard it is to find a job that is as exciting and influential as my TCinGC experience."

⊕

Knowing how to help, lead, and leave sustainable value in an organization is usually not clear to someone without this kind of experience. Most students' early work experiences are as entry-level employees. They are given clear directions on the definitions of their jobs and how to perform them.

For example, students who go unprepared into consulting assignments may assume the role of an information technology (IT) expert. Because they perceive that their responsibility is to solve an IT problem, they may focus solely on the technology, work as independently as possible, and create a purely technical solution. This is an "expert-for-hire" approach that is more appropriate for a technician than a consultant.

But TCinGC teaches students professional leadership and communication skills. It teaches them to use these skills to help solve organizational problems by using technology and to help clients more effectively carry out their missions. It emphasizes a different role for the student. The TCinGC consulting model focuses on working in partnership with a client to build capacity that will sustain innovation in the organization.

The students' work begins before they leave campus. They learn about the consulting model and begin researching the nation where they will be working. They work to understand the history and culture of their temporary home: history, local customs, holidays, taboos, a little of the local language, local cuisine, and safety concerns. And they attend to the myriad logistics necessary for international travel: passports, visas, immunizations, health insurance, and needed supplies. It's a little scary for one who hasn't traveled internationally. But it's good practice, especially for future professionals who will work in global markets.

Student consultants do not start with a clear scope of work or even a problem statement. Rather, they begin with what is often a very vague impression of what a client organization hopes to do. This requires the student consultant to broadly understand the organization and to bring clearer definition to the problems they face. It's the students' challenge to bring structure to the ambiguity and ultimately to define a scope of work. They need to show that they understand the organization and its problems, that they have considered the alternatives, and that they have arrived at a feasible and sustainable solution.

The consulting model starts with listening and observing. Our student consultants gather information broadly and refrain from jumping too soon to talking about solutions. They need to understand the mission of the organization, its history, and its place in the community. They need to understand who the staff members are and how comfortable they are in using technology. Technology, as a solution, is most often used to manage information and communication. But what information needs to be managed? Where are the current problem areas? And what are the current technology management and planning practices? To help answer questions like these, students are given a consulting roadmap and examples of how to use it.

As student consultants work through the summer on their projects, TCinGC faculty-advisors help them think through issues and options. The students' stories in this book describe the help they got from advisors. But ultimately a student consultant must step into the leadership position to articulate, communicate, and defend what he or she thinks is the best course of action.

This can be very challenging for young people. It's rare that they have previously needed to make and defend decisions that impact others, especially those who are senior to them in age, experience, and responsibility. But, as you have read, they rise to the task!

TCinGC's partner organizations usually cannot afford market-rate consulting, and our student consultants are available only for ten weeks. That's why we try not to create dependency but instead build sustainable capacity. The student consultant's goal is not to solve the problem *for* the client, but to work *with* the client to solve the problem in a way that creates a new capacity to sustain the solution after the consultant is gone. This consulting model works best when the client accepts the process, wants to understand and solve problems, and not just find someone to make the problem go away.

Our student consultants have worked in Africa, South America, Asia, the Pacific Islands, and even Alaska. Altogether, 76 students have worked on projects with 35 organizations in 14 developing nations around the world.

In an increasingly global world, we prepare students to build sustainable value as they work across cultures. They need to be able to go into a new culture and be effective quickly. This requires them to be adept at the practical logistics of foreign travel. They need skills to prepare for work in a new culture and to communicate across age, gender, language, and technical ability. And they need to work in ways that bring sustained value to their clients. These are all skills that cannot be taught in a classroom. Rather, they require students to face challenges and build their own skills. These experiences lead to knowledge that students can take into their personal and professional lives. The students develop confidence that will allow them to take risks, find opportunities, and work effectively in the global community.

www.ingramcontent.com/pod-product-compliance
Lightning Source LLC
Chambersburg PA
CBHW041257040426
42334CB00028BA/3061